Alden
1855

J. S. Burt,
Lane Seminary
Ohio.

BIBLICAL INTERPRETATION.

A

BRIEF TREATISE

ON THE

CANON AND INTERPRETATION

OF THE

HOLY SCRIPTURES:

FOR THE SPECIAL BENEFIT OF

JUNIOR THEOLOGICAL STUDENTS:

BUT INTENDED ALSO FOR PRIVATE CHRISTIANS IN GENERAL.

By ALEX. McCLELLAND,

PROFESSOR OF BIBLICAL LITERATURE IN THE THEOLOGICAL SEMINARY
AT NEW BRUNSWICK.

Second Edition, Enlarged.

NEW YORK:
ROBERT CARTER AND BROTHERS, 285 BROADWAY.
1850.

CONTENTS.

SPECIAL RULES.

RULE VII.

RULE VIII.

RULE IX.

RULE X.

RULE XI.

PREFACE.

The following work was drawn up with exclusive reference to the wants of the Junior Class in the Theological Seminary with which the author is connected, and was intended as a general introduction to the subject of which it treats. His design in publishing it, is to spare the young gentlemen some weary hours in writing imperfect and erroneous transcripts, while he thinks that it may be useful to others in their situation.

He has attempted to exhibit the subject he has undertaken to discuss, in a form so popular and devoid of technicality, that the student fresh from a literary institution can comprehend the whole in a few sittings, and make an immediate use of it in reading the Scriptures.

Part I. treats of their genuineness and canonical authority. That some preparation of this kind is proper and necessary, before entering on the study of them, will not be questioned. Every man, when he takes up a volume, should know with some degree of certainty—what it is, by whom written, and with what measure ot authority it addresses him. If this be true generally, how especially important in reference to a volume making such lofty claims as the Old and New Testaments! Our discussion of the subject is necessarily brief, but it will furnish the student with useful general ideas, on which he may at a future time, build a more complete and extensive edifice. On one point we may be thought needlessly diffuse, viz., the allegation of testimonies. But it was desirable to make a full and fair impression on the mind; and this could only be done, by spreading before it a considerable mass of authorities, in the very words of the writers. This has unavoidably given a dry and unpopular cast to the discussion: but we did not undertake to write a novel.

Part II. contains the principles and rules of interpretation. We have here also aimed at brevity, and condensation; but have not forgotten the necessity of guarding against obscurity, by appropriate illustrations. Young minds are not successfully addressed by dry apothegms and abstractions. *Cases* must be adduced, to give the lessons imparted—hue and coloring, and the form of composition should be that of continued argument, both to satisfy the understanding and impress the memory. Whether a happy selection of examples has been made, others must pronounce—not the author: they are, for the most part, such as occurred at the time of writing. With regard to the originality of the work, lofty pretensions to new discovery on so beaten a topic as the meaning of Scripture, would be extremely silly, and prove that the work is, in reality, worthless. Yet the intelligent reader will perceive, that I endeavor to do my own thinking on the different points—asking for the old paths, without surrendering private judgment, or anxiously keeping my wheel in another man's rut.

I have only to add, that there are scarcely three pages in the whole volume, so exclusively addressed to theological students, that the unlearned reader can derive no advantage from them. It is hoped therefore, that private Christians will not find their money thrown away in purchasing it. To them as well as to the ministry, our blessed Lord addresses the command, "Search the Scriptures;" and the manner of their performing the duty, will be a solemn item in the account which they must render.

The first edition of this work was exhausted long before the author determined on publishing a second. But he found so much relief by the use of it, from the intolerable drudgery connected with imparting orally to young men elementary information, that its continued use became almost neccessary. The present edition is greatly enlarged. But our worthy publisher assures us, that he will not greatly enlarge the price.

INTRODUCTION.

We are about to exhibit, in brief compass, evidence of the canonical authority of Holy Scripture, and rules by which the Christian student should be guided in the study of its contents. Before entering on the discussion, we are desirous of saying a few words, on the deep responsibility which those whom we specially address, are under, in relation to this matter. Mere rules, however clearly laid down and faithfully written on the tablets of memory, will be of little avail, unless accompanied with earnest, vigorous, and untiring labor in reducing them to practice. Allow us, then, young brethren, to speak on this point, with frankness and Christian affection. As candidates for the sacred office, you have a duty to perform to the word of God, which requires the devotion of your best faculties, the consecration of all your time, and a fixedness of purpose which nothing can relax. If you doubt it, look at the *nature of that office!*

Perhaps Christianity is in nothing more strikingly distinguished from other religions, than in the func-

originality of the work, lofty pretensions to new discovery on so beaten a topic as the meaning of Scripture, would be extremely silly, and prove that the work is, in reality, worthless. Yet the intelligent reader will perceive, that I endeavor to do my own thinking on the different points—asking for the old paths, without surrendering private judgment, or anxiously keeping my wheel in another man's rut.

I have only to add, that there are scarcely three pages in the whole volume, so exclusively addressed to theological students, that the unlearned reader can derive no advantage from them. It is hoped therefore, that private Christians will not find their money thrown away in purchasing it. To them as well as to the ministry, our blessed Lord addresses the command, "Search the Scriptures;" and the manner of their performing the duty, will be a solemn item in the account which they must render.

The first edition of this work was exhausted long before the author determined on publishing a second. But he found so much relief by the use of it, from the intolerable drudgery connected with imparting orally to young men elementary information, that its continued use became almost neccessary. The present edition is greatly enlarged. But our worthy publisher assures us, that he will not greatly enlarge the price.

INTRODUCTION.

WE are about to exhibit, in brief compass, evidence of the canonical authority of Holy Scripture, and rules by which the Christian student should be guided in the study of its contents. Before entering on the discussion, we are desirous of saying a few words, on the deep responsibility which those whom we specially address, are under, in relation to this matter. Mere rules, however clearly laid down and faithfully written on the tablets of memory, will be of little avail, unless accompanied with earnest, vigorous, and untiring labor in reducing them to practice. Allow us, then, young brethren, to speak on this point, with frankness and Christian affection. As candidates for the sacred office, you have a duty to perform to the word of God, which requires the devotion of your best faculties, the consecration of all your time, and a fixedness of purpose which nothing can relax. If you doubt it, look at the *nature of that office!*

Perhaps Christianity is in nothing more strikingly distinguished from other religions, than in the function and duties assigned to its ministers. The priests of heathenism, never dared to come out among the people, as simple promulgers of truth. Indeed they could not well give what was not in their possession, and this they knew. Not a philosopher of the porch or academy, laughed more heartily than themselves, at the ridiculous impostures they were daily practising on their votaries! What their system wanted in solidity, however, they made up in form, and if it could not speak to the understanding, it should at least dazzle the senses, and captivate the imagination. Hence those magnificent structures, whose broken fragments are still the world's admiration, in whose sacred shrines were encased the wonderful achievements of statuary—the all but breathing Gods of stone, which modern virtuosos still worship with little short of heathen idolatry. Hence the expensive sacrificial rites by which these marble gods were propitiated, the pompous festivals and processions, the magnificent exhibitions of poetry, dance, and song, which in their origin were purely religious, and never entirely lost the character of worship rendered to the Deity. Hence the famous mysteries, in the celebration of which everything was combined to awe—to fascinate—to bind in the chains of an abject superstition, the man who yielded himself to their bewitchments.

But far different is the spell, which our holy religion of light and love casts on the human faculties! Prejudice itself cannot deny, that whether its principles be true or false, they belong to a system magnificently intellectual. Far, indeed, are we from supposing, that its exclusive aim is to rectify speculative error: Its astonishing power over the heart, is a fact conceded by all. But we mean to say, that this control it exercises, through the previous mastery it has obtained over the understanding—the conscience—the unsophisticated sense of right and wrong. It calls to deep thoughts—grave discourse, soul-stirring contemplations. The themes which it brings before the mind, are so magnificent and enchained with infinity itself, that the sublimest intellect is lost, before it has entered on their investigation; and yet so congenial to reason, that what we do comprehend, appear almost self-evident propositions.

It tells concerning a pure Almighty Spirit, who, by a simple act of will, called into being the heavens and the earth. It imparts the most interesting details concerning his providential government, informs us of our primitive condition, and gives the most simple and beautiful solution of the great problem which has confounded the acutest minds, "whence come evils upon men." It tells us, when, and where, the first notice was given of that plan of mercy, into which angels are looking with growing wonder and delight. It relates with accuracy the preparatory measures for its execution, unfolding his mysterious dealings for more than a thousand years with that singular people, whom he had selected to be the depository of prophecy and promise, till the advent of *him*, in whom all families of the earth should be blessed. Thus far, we are only in the holy place of the temple—and now the veil is rent in twain, which concealed the glories of the inner house, allowing us to behold the *true ark* and the *living personal Shechinah*, "God manifested in the flesh;" who, after he had purged our sins, ascended on high, and sat down at the right hand of the heavenly majesty!

In exact correspondence with so thoughtful and suggestive a religion, is the work of its official minister. He is not a master of ceremonies, presiding over a splendid ritual, which fills the eye, but leaves an aching void in the heart. He is, by divine institution, a *teacher;* and in the simple, naked grandeur of this character, he stands before the people. A volume has been put into his hands of rich and various contents, nay, absolutely teeming with matter; and at the peril of his soul, he must spread it out in its whole length and breadth before his hearers. The principle on which he must act, is this simple and obvious one, and there is nothing in his commission which he may deliberately overlook. He is not at liberty here. Some parts of duty may perhaps be omitted without subjecting him to the brand of gross unfaithfulness. But if he neglects to expound the sacred volume, if he show no anxiety to form among his people, habits of carefully reading and inwardly digesting it, he may well tremble at the thought of rendering an account.

Labor then—labor, is heaven's first law of preparation for the gospel ministry. We have seen, that the Bible, though a popular, and in many respects an easy book, presents serious difficulties to him who would become master of its treasures. Both its great divisions, are written in languages, which have long ceased to be vernacular. The people who spoke them, were distinguished by remarkable peculiarities of opinion, habits, laws, which influenced greatly their modes of expression. Besides therefore, possessing a knowledge of Hebrew and Greek, one must be well acquainted with Jewish and classical antiquities, including chronology, geography, civil and religious history. Yet, even this is but preliminary. Now comes the actual tug: the reading of verse after verse with the accurate settling of every philological question that arises, by aid of the dictionary and grammar; the examining of scope, context, parallelism, idiom and tropical diction; the comparing our own results with those of some judicious commentator; and the careful gathering up of the great truths, whether doctrinal or practical, contained in every paragraph. These—are the gymnastics, by which the young Christian athlete learns to endure hardness, and becomes a skilful and gallant soldier in the service of his master! Do you complain of the arrangement? Then ask the Lord Jesus Christ, why he ordained it; why it was not enough to tread the "dolorous way" in his own person, without imposing vigils and self-denials on his followers? Tell him plainly, that while you like his wages, you dislike the labor; and wish to share his kingdom without companionship in his patience and tribulation. Does your cheek mantle with shame at the suggestion? Then be silent young man—and to your work!! It is quite honor enough for the disciple to be as his master, and the servant as his Lord.

But some one asks, in a tone half-apologetical, whether, after all, much of the trouble we have spoken of may not be spared? Are we not blessed with "king James' admirable translation of the Bible," and with most judicious commentators, in whom are reposited as much criticism and literary information, as are necessary to a right understanding it? Why, as the fountain is so difficult of access, not content ourselves with these delectable pipes at our very door? We confess, that language like this, when heard, (as it sometimes is) ruffles our good humor. God, in his infinite kindness to men, has preserved for them an ample revelation of his will, by a series of dispensations falling little short of miracle. He has set apart an order of men to be its official expounders, and the church is generously sustaining the institution by its munificent provision for the gratuitous education of candidates in all stages of their progress, and when they have entered on their work, by relieving them from every worldly care and avocation, that they may give themselves wholly to it, and their profiting may appear to all men. Yet the question is seriously asked, whether a practical acquaintance with these lively oracles in their proper dialects, should be anxiously cultivated by the Christian minister!!

We blush to think in how many respects, the children of the world are wiser than the children of light. The merchant's clerk, if his interest point that way, will sit down and master French, Spanish and German, without heaving a sigh. The gentleman who intends to travel a few years in the East, grudges no pains to make himself acquainted with Turkish, Arabic, or Lingua Franca. Even the girl scarcely in her teens, wearied of thrumming on her guitar to the harsh strains of her native English, determines, and carries the purpose through in a way that might astonish many a grave student of the other sex, to achieve a conquest over the sweetly-flowing Italian. But the professed interpreter of God's holy word, the legate of the skies, is so astounded at the thought of learning effectively a pair of languages—than either of which, a finer never vibrated on the human ear, that he prefers to live and die, just able to spell the letters of his commission!

With regard to our English translation, much as we admire that noble monument of "English pure and undefiled," which will last probably as long as the world; we say to those who quote it in the present argument, that it is an exceedingly imperfect representation of the original. The venerable men who formed it, were not profoundly versed in either Greek or Hebrew, though their attainments were eminent for the day in which they lived; and accordingly, there are not a few instances in every page, where the sense is not injured merely, but entirely lost. Even where the signification of words is given properly, the transitive and connecting particles which show the relation of the different members of a thought, have secondary meanings, so entirely different from those of the corresponding particles in English, that a literal version is often nothing better than a mere travesty of the original. Take St. Paul for an example. It is quite impossible for a mere English reader to peruse his argumentative epistles, without feeling tempted to suspect, that there may be a grain of truth in the profane remark of Dr. Priestly, that his premises are not always sound, nor his conclusions logical. His reverence for inspiration, will not allow him to say so in express words. But if asked the question, he will acknowledge his great surprise at the little profit which he receives, from the decidedly most intellectual writer of the Christian school.

Now where in this doubt and darkness shall the interpreter go? To expositors? But expositors often differ; and who shall decide when doctors disagree? The value of this class of authors to the unlearned reader, and to the learned also, if properly used, we are far from denying. But not one is to be absolutely trusted. To none, does the remark of Mr. Locke that "every man has a secret flaw in his cranium, producing some extravagancy in opinion or action, which in that particular renders him fitter for Bedlam than ordinary conversation," apply with more force than to commentators. The best has not only faults, but frequently under the influence of sectarian bias or mental idiosyncracy, fall into perfect absurdity. He only therefore uses them with safety, who can compare them together, and exercise an eclectic judgment of his own. Pitiable, most pitiable, is the condition of that professed teacher of Christianity, the only source of illumination to whose darkened mind, are the contradictory opinions of men—who has not the shadow of a reason for his preference of one above another, except that it is more agreeable to the Shibboleth of his sect!

Can a creature thus lame, blind, and shackled, the passive recipient of whatever the adopted lord of his understanding and conscience may choose to impose upon him, be called an authoritative (we grant the "authorized") expounder of divine truth? Impossible! and no one is more fully convinced of it than the man himself. He may not run to the house-top and proclaim it: for this would greatly lower his estimation with the people, and probably something else. He may even join in the senseless clamor against a learned ministry. But he feels nevertheless, that he labors under a dreadful *incompetency*, that he is a *blind leader of the blind*, right only by *chance*, and without even enjoying the happiness of knowing it; that the noblest part of him, his understanding, is prostrate before a miserable creature *as blind perhaps as himself*, whom he often suspects, but *always follows*—with the servility of a dog, not daring to move a hand-breadth from his track. In a word, he cannot help despising himself, and takes refuge probably from the shame of his own thoughts, in the entire neglect of scriptural inquiries—limiting his ambition to ringing peals from Sabbath to Sabbath, on a few topics of general exhortation!

These remarks may be thought more applicable to those already in the sacred office, than persons who are in a course of preparation. But it is not so. Though the evil is developed in the ministry, its birthplace and cradle are our seminaries of learning. Here, those habits are formed both for good and evil, which mould the character beyond the reach of change, except by the sovereign grace of God. We fear that they are often formed *badly;* and that many of our young candidates for the ministry need the application of a little stimulus to their reason and conscience.

The general sincerity of their purpose to serve God faithfully in the Gospel of his Son, we do not intend here to question. But that they are far from being awake to the necessity of vigorous and untiring effort, in making biblical preparation for their work, is too evident. They entered the Theological seminary, perhaps, full of life and ardor. But alas! in one short month, a chilling frost came over them, nipping the tender buds of promise, and infusing a deadly torpor through all their faculties. They became fatigued —alarmed—and are evidently disappointed men. They seem to have expected, that after passing through the strait gate of conversion, they should be put on a road strewed with flowers, bordered with groves of citron—and couches of ease at every turn, inviting the traveller to sweet repose. 'Tis hard, they think—passing hard, that gentlemen of talent and piety, so devoted to the great work of converting sinners, that if the church permitted it, they would gladly mount the pulpit at once, should be treated almost as harshly as a galley-slave at the oar; condemned to disinter a thousand Hebrew roots, analyze a legion of Hellenistic idioms, pore over Latin, Greek, Oriental Antiquities; and be told that when all this is accomplished, preparation for their work may be considered fairly begun!

The effect of such reflections is apparent. They have become listless, inert, melancholy. Study does not agree with their constitution; producing dyspepsia, palpitations of the heart, "incipient bronchitis," and a determination of blood to the head. A hundred times in the day they exclaim, what a weariness is it! and gladly seek relief in dull vacuity of thought, idle miscellaneous reading, or talking pretty nothings in a lady's parlor. Perhaps to make time pass less heavily, they offer their preaching services to a neighboring prayer-meeting, where the plaudits received, give precious omen of more extensive triumphs, and prove, that genius like theirs, may safely despise the uncouth adornments of Greek and Hebrew. Many of them deem the irksome season of probation, an admirable time for securing that best of earthly blessings—*a good wife;* and thus, a business in which the wisest man is apt to play the fool, they contrive to despatch, at the period when every faculty, every affection of their being, should be engrossed by the one great object which has received their consecration! This impatience of labor, this morbid desire to engage in an enterprise without submitting to wholesome preparatory discipline, this voluptuous effeminacy of character, is a blight and a curse on all our seminaries of learning.*

All, are not thus. We attest it with pleasure, and even fully believe, that could a census be taken, the

* Yet the evil is attributable far more to our literary institutions, than to the young men themselves. The truth is, they have had no opportunity of obtaining suitable preparation, or forming proper habits: We speak at present of the study of languages. They are sent to schools, whose reputation has been established by the magical rapidity with which they turn out finished scholars to the various colleges in their neighborhood; and when in college, they admirably succeed in losing the scanty modicum which they acquired in school. The writer has heard scores of ingenuous youth confess with bitter regret, that their whole course in Alma Mater was a regular business of forgetting the little Greek they had previously acquired.

class described above, would be found in a decided minority. There are many, however, who cherish an honest wish and purpose to do their duty, yet are not a little daunted by the prospect before them. It seems to stretch out into immensity! Is adequate preparation, they ask, feasible? Are they capable of attaining by conscientious exertion, such a real acquaintance with the languages and literature of Scripture, that on their entering the ministry and applying to the work of exposition, the painful thought will not obtrude, that they have been laboring to no valuable purpose? Assuming, that those who put the question, commence their theological course, possessing that amount of learning which ought to be obtained in a literary college, we answer, Yes! With the ordinary blessing of Him, whose you are, and whom you serve, it depends entirely *on yourselves.* We do not affect to conceal the difficulties which are in the way. The elementary exercises of learning the grammar and vocabulary of a strange language, of impressing on the memory the genders, cases, and other accidents of nouns, of hunting verbs through all the mazes of conjugation, we admit, were not exactly the form, in which Satan presented the temptation to aspire after knowledge in Paradise. But what then? Would you expect young men to be placed above the universal law of heaven, that every thing truly valuable, is purchased by strenuous exertion?

Far however be the thought, that Preparation is in

all its stages a painful drudgery. Only let the student sit down, and make a fair trial: he will be astonished to find how soon light rises out of darkness, and the impediments which seemed insurmountable disappear, until his path becomes agreeable, and even delightful. The forms of words, with their significations, gradually rivet themselves in his memory, so that he can recall them with ease and pleasure. His dictionary enjoys longer intervals of rest; the beauties of thought and expression begin to show themselves, like modest daisies in spring—and what a blessed rapture pours its tide through his soul, when he discovers that he can draw the water of salvation directly from the limpid fountain, and with his own hand pluck the healing leaves from the tree of life! Then his work goes on pleasantly indeed! A field of delightful employment stretches before him—a garden of the Lord, lovelier than Eden ever was, which he cultivates without pain, whose fruit he gathers without fatigue, while the God who placed him there, walks amid the foliage, and converses with him face to face.

This is no fancy sketch. Those who have gone through the process, will certify to the truth of every word, and say that after a certain stage of progress, the critical reading of Holy Scripture became one of the most pleasant occupations of their life. Witness the beautiful recital of the learned and pious Bishop Horne of his state of mind, while preparing his Commentary on the Psalms.—"Could the author flatter himself," he says "that any one would take half the pleasure in reading the following exposition, which he has taken in writing it, he would not fear the loss of his labor. The employment detached him from the bustle and hurry of life, the din of politics, and noise of folly. Vanity and vexation flew away for a season, care and disquietude came not near his dwelling. He arose fresh as the morning to his task, the silence of night invited him to pursue it, and he can truly say that food and rest were not preferred before it. Happier hours than those which have been spent on these meditations on the songs of Zion, he never expects to see in this world. Very pleasantly did they pass, and moved smoothly and swiftly along; for when thus engaged he counted no time. They are gone, but have left a relish and fragrance on the mind, and the remembrance of them is sweet." Will you not feel encouraged, young friends and brethren, by this experience of the venerable bishop, to enter on your work like men? Away with despondency and forebodings of defeat. Away with that ingenuity, which, bribed by indolence, sees monsters and lions in the way. Listen not to those evil spies, those lazy, worthless cowards, who would tell you that the good land which flows with milk and honey, is beset with giants, sons of Anak; that the Amalekites dwell in the south, Hittites, Jebusites, and Amorites, in the mountains, the Canaanites by the sea; and that you cannot go against this people! Hear them not, but say in the strength of the Lord, and your own firm purpose, "Let us go up to possess it, for we are fully able to overcome them." You will not be uttering a vain boast. Victory is certain, and when it comes, you will be more than recompensed for all your toils.

Pardon us, if we dwell a moment longer on this subject, and remind you what the recompense will be. Are you anxious that one day you may cover with confusion the bold infidel, who defies the armies of the living God, and by calm convincing demonstrations, which shall come home to the honest understandings of men, show the groundlessness of his objections? This, you will be able to do, by displaying the truth, beauty and moral dignity of that blessed volume against which his violence is directed—in order to which, you *must have studied it.* Without study, you will scarcely be able to avert the baneful influence of scepticism from your own soul, much less build your hearers on their most holy faith. Do you wish to become vivid, interesting, various preachers, who make their hearers *feel* the commanding energy of truth, and whom they never tire of hearing, as every sermon brings forth new evidences of apostleship? Study your Bible! There, you will find inexhaustible resources of pleasing, impressing, profiting. Prepare yourselves for expounding the word of God, from Sabbath to Sabbath. Prepare yourselves for bringing before the people, Moses and the Prophets, Christ and his Apostles, to unfold its instructive histories, analyze its charming parables, disentangle and develop its sublime reasonings. If such be the character of your exhibitions, we venture to promise you immunity against one sore evil under the sun—that of being waited on by a church session or consistory, in the second year of your labors, and affectionately informed, that there is no farther call for your services.

Do you wish to be eminently successful in winning souls to Christ? Study THE BOOK. This, is the two-edged sword, that pierces to the dividing asunder of soul and spirit, joints and marrow, and is a discerner of the thoughts and intents of the heart. Machinery has been invented, which, worked by skilful hands, can furnish to order a greater number of nominal converts, manufactured in a given period; but "the truth" alone, makes children of God and heirs of immortality!

Have you regard to personal comfort and enjoyment? What an inexhaustible source of amusement —yes, amusement, high and holy as that of angels, will you possess, when you have acquired the taste, skill, and habit, of reading in its originals, the holy Word. To this mount you will be able to retire at any moment, like the pious Horne, from the cares and turmoils of life, and see more than the three disciples saw, on the hallowed summit of Tabor. When afflicted and almost repining at the ways of Heaven, let your old Hebrew Bible introduce you to the bedside of venerable Job, with whom and his friends, you may speculate on the mysteries of Providence, until convicted of your folly, you join with him in his humble acknowledgment, "I have uttered what I understood not, things too wonderful which I knew not!" Are you suffering under hypochondriac depression? you may order the sweet singer of Israel to strike his lyre: If its music does not expel the evil spirit, as it did from Saul, your case is indeed melancholy.

But the study we recommend, will be far more than an occasional solace. The preparation of a series of expository remarks on an important portion of Scripture, which he knows his people look for on the ensuing Sabbath, furnishes to a pastor a delightful regular employment, that rouses the faculties, gives elasticity to every muscle, fillips the blood, and is more conducive to health than all the medicine of the dispensatory. We are not ignorant, that mental application is considered by many unfavorable to a good condition of the physical system, and that by this supposed fact, they explain the meagre and hectic looks of clergymen. Nothing is more absurd. Look through the world, and you will find no class of men more vigorous and long-lived than active thinkers. The truth is, clergymen do not study enough. That they sit much, and are more sequestered from the hum and tumult of society than members of other professions, is fully granted. But *sitting* is not *studying*, nor are we willing to bestow this respectable name on the mechanical operation of transposing a few stale thoughts, repeated a thousand times, on certain common-places of Didactic Theology. What the ministry need, is an employment bringing them in contact with a succession of new as well as interesting objects, which will produce an agreeable tension of the faculties, never wearying, or followed by reaction, because sustained by a constant and pleasing variety. Such, you will find to be the regular study and exposition of sacred Scripture. It will do thee good like a medicine, and be "marrow to thy bones."

In view of all these motives, we pray you, as a friend and brother, as one who every day looks back with regret to his own misimprovement of youthful privileges, to exert untiring diligence in biblical preparation for your work. Systems of human concoction have their use: but they are of secondary importance. As such, must you view them. You *must get close up* to the pure crystal fountain, that issues from the heavenly throne. There, you must dwell; thence must you draw, for your own souls, and the souls of those committed to your charge. "Blessed is the servant, who, when the Master comes, shall be found so doing."

PART I.

GENUINENESS AND CANONICAL AUTHORITY OF THE SCRIPTURES.

CHAPTER I.

OF THE NEW TESTAMENT.

THE divine Author of our religion, intending that it should be a perpetual blessing to the human race, among other provisions for accomplishing his purpose, took care that it should be committed to writing. Had this not been done, the most fatal consequences would have ensued. It is absurd to suppose, that oral tradition could preserve so great a number of doctrines and facts as Christianity is made up of, in their original integrity. They would have been lost, or disguised and altered; and nothing but an interposition like that which raised Lazarus from the grave, would have saved our holy and beautiful temple from being utterly desecrated, and perhaps (as the Catholic experiment has proved) made the cage of every hateful and unclean bird. It was therefore essential, that the great objects of faith should be recorded on enduring tablets, accessible to all mankind. The scattered rays of truth thus became collected into a focus, and religion received that fixed and unchangeable character, which became a revelation from God.

To this, and this alone, it owes its continued existence. It survived the furious assaults of Pagan Rome; which crushed the persons of its disciples, but was utterly foiled in the attempt to exterminate its writings. The volume of volumes continued to circulate. It entered the hovel and the palace, it stole into the camp, it might be found stowed away under the senatorial robe; and history tells us, that long before the time of Constantine—while Paganism sat enthroned without even thinking of a rival, it had forced its way into the imperial palace. It is this, too, which gives our religion that wonderful power of *reproduction*, by which it can emerge to light and liberty, after ages of declension. When the mighty man of Wirtemberg, with his friends and coadjutors, undertook to purify the church from those corruptions, which she had suffered so long, that the knowledge of a better state had passed away from the memory of man—all necessary to be done, was the emancipation of the written word. The moment an appeal was made to its decisions, and men learned to compare them with the sad realities that surrounded them—Popery received a wound, which, though not immediately fatal, doomed it to a lingering decay, and certain death, when the purposes of God shall be completed.

It is called by various names; which we pass over, to consider that which more immediately concerns the present discussion.

DEFINITION OF THE WORDS "CANON" AND "CANONICAL."

The word "Canon," is derived from the Greek κανων, —which properly denotes the beam of a balance, and also a rule by which anything is tried and determined. At an early period, it was employed to signify a catalogue of articles belonging to the church; all questions of property being decided by an appeal to such catalogues. Soon, it became yet more restricted in its meaning; being applied almost exclusively, to a publicly approved catalogue of the books which were received by Christians, as the productions of inspired men. "They fall into great absurdities," says Chrysostom, "who will not follow the Canon of Scripture, but trust to their own reasoning." "Only in the Canonical writings," says Athanasius, "is the instruction which blesses imparted; they only are the fountains of saving knowledge."

It will be proper to define, with a little more precision, the ideas attached by the Christian Fathers to this word, and the kind of writing to which it was applied.

In the first place, they required that a book be the production of an Apostle, or Apostolic man. To Apostles only, did our Lord promise the Spirit of revelation. As to Mark and Luke, who were not of the number—the former was the kinsman and pupil of Peter, who communicated all the facts recorded in his Gospel. Luke was the friend and associate of Paul, who exercised over him an inspection like that which Peter exercised over Mark. They were therefore from the earliest period recognized as men "apostolical," and their works universally received as part of the Canon.

The second distinction of a canonical book, was its being publicly read in the assemblies of the faithful. This was done in imitation of the Jews; whose synagogue worship mainly consisted in reciting portions of their Scriptures, to which they gave the name of "Paraschoth" and "Haphtaroth." The meanest Christian, thus became acquainted with the great truths of his religion. The names and number of the books, became as familar to all, as the names and number of the members of their families, and the strongest safeguard that can be imagined, was provided against unauthentic productions. Indeed it seemed hardly possible under such circumstances, to impose a spurious composition.

The third peculiarity of these writings, was their *binding authority* as a rule of faith and practice. This followed from the first, by necessary consequence:

For if they were truly the productions of men to whom Christ had promised the inspiring Spirit, they could not but express the will of the divine Being, without any mixture of error. Accordingly, they were universally appealed to as the fountains of all saving truth. "Our assertions and discourses," says Origen, "are unworthy of credit. We must receive the Scripture as witnesses." "In all doubtful cases," says Cyprian, "we must go to the fountain. If the truth has in any way been shaken, recur to the Gospels, and apostolic writings." Even the Arians appealed to this touchstone; arguing against the phrases used by the Orthodox concerning the Trinity, that they were not in the Scriptures: and one of them thus addresses St. Augustine: "If you say what is reasonable, I must submit. If you allege anything from the divine Scripture, I must hear—but unscriptural expressions deserve no regard."

These, are the ideas comprehended in the word Canon, or Canonical writing; the first of which, is doubtless the primary and fundamental one. Let the fact be established, that the books of the New Testament proceeded from inspired and apostolic men, and it is explained at once, why they were publicly read in the churches, and regarded as the infallible rule of faith and practice.

STATEMENT OF THE QUESTION.

These preliminaries being settled—the question fairly presents itself: *Have we solid grounds for believing, that our books, as found in the common English Testament, were written and published to the world eighteen hundred years ago, by the venerated founders of Christianity to whom they are ascribed;* or were they fabricated at a later period, by some artful impostor? We assert the first position; and deny the second. We say, that there is an unbroken chain of evidence, commencing with contemporary writers, and extending to the present time—writers, who enjoyed every opportunity of knowing the truth, and whose character for veracity is unimpeachable, that our volume is the work of nine primitive disciples of Christ, and has been always received as the complete exponent of his system, whose decisions are final on every point.

It is scarcely necessary to add to the statement, and yet it may prevent some confusion of ideas, that our inquiry does not regard immediately the *credibility* of the document, or its *divine inspiration.* The persons whom we address, are assumed to be—not infidels—but young Christian disciples; who, entering on the study of a volume which professes to contain the principles of their faith, are desirous of knowing the grounds on which it rests its claim—of knowing, for instance, where it came from, by whom it was received, and at how early a period. Whether Christianity in its essential principles—viewed as a power, or germ of a new moral life, came from God, we suppose to be settled; and now the question comes up, which we desire to aid them in answering, whether there is anything in the parentage of this little volume, and the manner in which it has been received and treated in all ages, which entitles it to address believers in the system, with commanding authority as its interpreter. In a word, our argument goes to show, that if they acknowledge the divine mission of Jesus—*this, is their book.*

The evidence, divides itself into—the testimony of Christians themselves, or, as some choose to express themselves, the "Church;" which must be supposed to know with perfect accuracy, what she received, from whom, and at what period: that of heretics, and Pagan infidels: and the *internal* marks of genuineness, so wonderfully striking, that were the books drawn from the bottom of a river and exposed to view for the first time, a cultivated scholar would pronounce them, confidently, to be the work of their alleged authors.

It would be quite impossible to discuss the whole of so rich a subject, in the few pages which we can devote to it. All proposed, therefore, is to furnish the reader with some useful information on the first, and principal topic, viz., the early and continued attestation of the Christian Church. The omission, however, can be justified only by the necessity referred to; for the testimony of heretics and infidels is exceedingly valuable. Beside the concessions of Ebionites and Gnostics of every hue, none of whom with all their fantastic mutilations, denied the genuineness of the writings, we have the concessions of heathen enemies, as bitter as any that appeared before the tribunal of Pilate—who, while they denied the truth of the New Testament, fully acknowledged its Apostolic origin. This precious confession runs through all their discourses, and it is a confession, that more than atones for the mischief they wrought. It has changed their spiteful calumnies and curses into positive blessings, so that our divine religion, which commands us "in every thing to give thanks," is enabled to illustrate, in the most remarkable way, its own precept—by thanking God for a Porphyry, a Julian, and a Celsus. The internal evidence, as we have already stated, is equally overwhelming. No volume in the world, of the same age, has half so much. No volume can advance such proof of its being written at the time and place alleged, and by the men whose name it bears—from its peculiar language, style, and mode of thinking on every subject; the minute circumstantiality of its narratives; the accuracy of its political, geographical, and historical references; the air of truth, and reality that pervades it; and the numberless fine coincidences between its different and most widely separated parts—all found, on careful examination, to be in perfect harmony with each other, and yet, such, as would never be thought of by a forger, though Satan himself were at his elbow. In short, it is *inimitable*—resembling that fine, delicately-tinted paper, used for certain purposes, which is of such exquisite texture, that no skill, even of the manufacturer himself can produce the like; and the genuineness of which, the practiced eye can perceive at once, by simply *holding it up to the sun.*

These, with their kindred topics, we wave for the reason mentioned, and proceed to our main object; premising, that nothing more must be looked for, than a meager specimen of the evidence. The quotations are extracted from the immense collection of the learned and accurate Lardner, with a few additions from his German continuators.

TESTIMONIES,* &C.

It is unnecessary to follow the subject below the fourth century, as the existence of our Canon at that time is perfectly established and indisputable. In stating the evidence, we take our position in the fourth century, and ascend to the 1st, herein differing from Dr. L.; because it is more natural to proceed from what is certain to what is obscure, than in a contrary direction. The notices of the

---

* There is a fact relative to the Canon, which readers should be acquainted with, before they enter on the examination of witnesses, that they may not experience a disagreeable shock. From very early times, a marked distinction was made in the Christian Church, between those books which were universally received as genuine, and others on which opinion was divided; in consequence of their wanting the clear, commanding evidence, possessed by the former. They were not proscribed, nor positively branded with the name of *Apocrypha*, but their

very early (Apostolical) fathers are so imperfect, that they would make little impression by themselves; but when the light of the following ages is reflected on them, they become a highly satisfactory part of the evidence.

IV. CENTURY.

COUNCIL OF NICE, A. D. 325.

This famous Assembly is introduced here, not to give its testimony, but to acknowledge that it *has none* to give. The notion that the Nicene Synod fixed the Canon of Scripture or in any way contributed to it by its deliberations and acts, is a pure fiction which has found favor with some, because it seemed to countenance their theory, that we have received the Canon of Scripture from the *Church;* and which infidels in their turn have seized upon to bolster up *their* favorite maxim, that our present catalogue is not the work of candid investigation, but ecclesiastical enactment.

There is not the least reason to believe that the subject ever came before the Council; most certainly, it was never acted on. The universal reception of certain books and exclusion of others, was the result of honest conviction, founded on a careful examination of what had been handed down from the wise of former times. Their genuineness was regarded as a *historical fact,* to be

---

claim was doubted, on the ground that they were rarely quoted by the more ancient Fathers. The following books belong to this class: The epistles of James, and Jude, the 2d of Peter, the 2d and 3d of John, the epistle to the Hebrews, and Revelation. They were called the "Controverted" books (αντιλεγομενα), the others being styled the "universally acknowledged" (ωμολογουμενα). That the hesitation felt concerning them was without solid reasons, seems probable from the fact that it gave way to a thorough investigation; as no trace of the distinction, is found after the fourth century. That it should exist before the scrutiny, was perfectly natural, and proves the anxious care with which Christians guarded their sacred catalogues against impure mixtures. There is no reason, therefore, why we should feel uncomfortable, at discovering in some of the testimonies quoted, what otherwise might be thought and called a "hiatus valde deflendus." This very hiatus, silences one of the worst calumnies of infidelity.

proved exactly as the genuineness of other documents; and so they did prove it, without fear of Synods and Synodical fulminations. The fact, that a majority of the witnesses were of the clerical order, is a *mere circumstance*, in no way affecting the nature of their testimony. They certify the universal reception, simply as individuals who have faithfully examined the subject; and their certificate would be quite as valuable, if every one of them had belonged to the laity. Doubtless it would have been more so, as the charge could not be made in this case, of interested motives and combination.

Those persons who talk of our receiving the Canon of Scripture from the "Church," in some mysterious way, as if the genuineness could not or ought not to be proved in the same manner with any other fact in History, seem to forget very strangely, that a most important part of the evidence is furnished by heretics and heathen enemies,—by men, in short, whom the church disowns and abhors. It may seem paradoxical to some, but it is perfectly true, that if the Lord Jesus Christ had never instituted a visible community, called a "church," on the earth, but had left his religion to operate by the mere force of its principles on individual minds, the evidence for the genuineness and apostolicity of the New Testament would scarcely be *in the least affected by* it.

No less than ten Catalogues of the books of the New Testament by writers of this age, have come down to us; all perfectly agreeing with our own, except that a few omit the Hebrews and Revelation.

AUGUSTINE—FLOURISHED A. D. 395.

After enumerating the books of the Old Testament, he proceeds thus—"Of the New, there are the four books of the gospel—according to Matthew, Mark, Luke, John; fourteen epistles of the Apostle Paul to the Romans, two to the Corinthians, to the Galatians, Ephesians, Phillipians, two to the Thessalonians, to the Colossians, two to Timothy, to Titus, Philemon, the Hebrews; two epistles of Peter, three of John, one of Jude, and one of James; the

Acts of the Apostles in one book; and the Revelation of John in one book. In these books, they who fear God seek his will."

"None can forbear observing," says Dr. Lardner, "how clean a catalogue here is of the books of the New Testament."

ATHANASIUS, A. D. 326.

"The books of the New Testament are these—the four Gospels according to Matthew, Mark, Luke, John. Then after them the Acts of the Apostles, and the seven epistles of the Apostles, called Catholic; of James, one, Peter, two, John, three, Jude, one. Besides these, there are the fourteen epistles of the Apostle Paul, the order of which is thus: the first, to the Romans, then, two to the Corinthians, that to the Galatians, the next, to the Ephesians, then, to the Phillipians, to the Colossians, two to the Thessalonians, the epistle to the Hebrews, two to Timothy, to Titus one, the last to Philemon, and again the Revelation of John. These are the fountains of salvation, that he who thirsts may be satisfied with the oracles contained in them: in these alone, the doctrine of religion is taught: let no man add to them or take any thing from them."

In his writings, he quotes all our books.

JEROME, A. D. 322.

He names and describes *all* the writers of the New Testament. "The first are Matthew. Mark, Luke, John, the chariot of the Lord, and the true cherubim, who go wherever the spirit leads them. The Apostle Paul writes to seven churches; for the eighth, that of the Hebrews, by many is not reckoned among them. He likewise instructs Timothy and Titus, and intercedes with Philemon for a runaway servant. The Acts of the Apostles, another work of Luke the Physician, whose praise is in the Gospel, contain the history of the infancy of the church. The apostles James, Peter, John, Jude, write seven epistles, of few words, but full of sense: the Revelation of John has as many mysteries as words." Jerome published a Latin translation of the New Testament containing precisely our books.

EUSEBIUS, A. D. 315.

"It will be proper to enumerate here in a summary way, the books of the New Testament which have been already mentioned. And in the first place, are to be ranked the sacred four Gospels: then, the Acts of the Apostles: after that, the epistles of Paul. In the next place, that, called the first epistle of John and the [first] epistle of Peter are to be esteemed authentic. After these, is to be placed, if it be thought fit, the Revelation of John, about which we shall observe the different opinions at a proper season. Of the *controverted*, but yet well known or *approved by the most*, are that called the epistle of James, and that of Jude, and the second of Peter, and the second and third of John; whether they are written by the evangelist, or another of the same name. Among the *spurious*, are to be placed the Acts of Paul, and the book entitled the Shepherd, and the Revelation of Peter: and besides these that called the epistle of Barnabas, and the book named the Doctrines of the Apostles. And moreover, as I said, the Revelation of John, if it seem meet, which some reject, others reckon among the books universally received."

There is some obscurity in this statement which has given trouble to critics, but the essential facts are clearly stated.

III. CENTURY.

Two formal catalogues have come down to us. But Dr. Lardner quotes *forty* writers who give ample testimony to our present Canon.

CYPRIAN, A. D. 248.

He mentions the four Gospels by the names of their authors, comparing them "to the four rivers of Paradise." By them the "Church is watered, and her plants are enabled to bear fruit." Dr. Lardner extracts from him at length quotations from *Acts, Rom.* I. and II. *Cor. Gal. Eph. Phil. Col. Thess. Tim. Tit.*—in short,—*all* Paul's epistles except the Hebrews. He also quotes 1st Peter and 1st John, and the Revelation often. There is not in Cyprian *one quotation from any apocryphal writer.*

VICTORINUS, A. D. 290.

In his commentary on the Revelation, he speaks of the four Gospels thus—"The four living creatures (Rev. iv. 6,) are the four Gospels. These living creatures have different faces, which have a meaning; for the living creature like a lion, denotes Mark, in whom the voice of a lion roaring in the wilderness is heard: "A voice crying in the wilderness, Prepare ye the way of the Lord." Matthew, who has the resemblance of a man, show sthe family of Mary, from whom Christ took flesh. Luke, who relates the priesthood of Zacharias offering sacrifice for the people, because of the priesthood and the mention of the sacrifice, has the resemblance of a calf. The evangelist John, like an eagle with stretched-out wings mounting on high, speaks the Word of God.'

Dr. Lardner shows, that he must have read all Paul's epistles except the Hebrews, of which he makes no mention. On the Revelation, *he wrote a Commentary.*

ORIGEN, A. D. 230.

"As I have learned by tradition concerning the four Gospels, which *alone are received without dispute by the whole church of God* under heaven. The first was written by Matthew, once a publican, afterwards an apostle of Jesus Christ. The second is that according to Mark, who wrote it as Peter dictated it to him. The third is that according to Luke, published for the sake of the Gentile converts. Lastly, that according to John. Paul did not write to all the churches he had taught; and to those, to which he did write, he sent only a few lines. Peter has left one epistle [universally] acknowledged. But let it be granted likewise that he wrote a second; for it is doubted of. But what need I speak of John, who leaned upon the breast of Jesus, who has left us one Gospel. He wrote also the Revelation. He has also left an epistle of a very few lines. Grant also a second and a third; for all do not allow these to be genuine."

In another place he speaks thus: "Matthew sounds first with his priestly trumpet in his gospel; Mark also, and Luke, and John, sounded with their priestly trumpets. Peter likewise sounds aloud with the two trumpets of his epistles; James also, and Jude. And John sounds again with his trumpet in his epistles, and the Revelation; and Luke also once more relating the actions of the apostles. Last of all comes Paul, and sounding with the trumpets of his fourteen epistles, he threw down to the foundations the walls of Jericho, and all the engines of idolatry; and the schemes of the philosophers."

Origen's quotations from the New Testament are so numerous that they form a volume.

AN UNKNOWN WRITER QUOTED BY MURATORI IN HIS "ITALIC ANTIQUITIES."—205.

Who he was, is unknown. Many suppose him to be Caius, a distinguished writer who flourished at the close of the 2d century. Muratori has inserted in his work, a Catalogue by this author of the New Testament books. Of its extreme antiquity, there can be no doubt. It is certainly not later, (according to Hug,) than the close of the second century. Being written by a member of the Roman Church, (evidently however, from a Greek original,) the language is Latin, and somewhat barbarous. The text also is corrupt: but the main facts are clearly stated. It contains the four Gospels, thirteen epistles of Paul, (omitting the Hebrews), Jude, two epistles, of John, probably one of Peter, (though the text is here corrupt,) and the Revelation.

II. CENTURY.

TERTULLIAN, A. D. 200.

Of the Gospels, he says: "We lay this down for a *certain* truth, that the evangelic Scriptures, have for their authors the Apostles, to whom the work of publishing the Gospel was committed by the Lord himself. Among the apostles, John and Matthew teach us the faith: among apostolical men Luke and Mark refresh it." This passage shows at once the number of the Gospels universally received, and the names of their authors, Matthew, Mark, Luke, and John.

Of the Epistles, he says :—"Let us then see, what milk the Corinthians received from Paul: to what rule the Galatians were reduced: what the Philippians read; what the Thessalonians, the Ephesians, and likewise what the Romans recite, who are near to us; with whom both Peter and Paul left the Gospel sealed with their blood. We have also churches which are the disciples of John; for though Marcion rejects his Revelation, *the succession of bishops traced up to the beginning* will show it to have John for its author." Accordingly, in his writings he quotes largely from Rom. Cor. Eph. Gal. Col. Thess. Tim. Titus, 1 Peter, 1 John, Jude, and Revelation.

There is a remarkable passage in his writings, that reads thus :—"Well, if you be willing to exercise your curiosity profitably in the business of your salvation, visit the apostolical churches, in which the very chairs of the apostles, still preside; in which their very *authentic* letters are recited sounding forth the voice, and representing the countenance, of each one of them. Is Achaia near you? You have Corinth. If you are not far from Macedonia, you have Phillippi, you have Thessalonica. If you can go to Asia, you have Ephesus. But if you are near to Italy, you have Rome, from whence we may also be easily satisfied."

What he means by the "authentic letters" of the Apostles, which he says have been deposited with the churches, is disputed. But it certainly establishes the fact, that correct copies if not the originals were laid up in the sacred libraries of the churches referred to, and were open to examination.

CLEMENS ALEXANDRINUS, A. D. 194.

Dr. Lardner, after an elaborate array of quotations by this writer from the New Testament, thus sums up his testimony. "He has expressly owned the four Gospels of Matthew, Mark, Luke, and John, and the Acts of the Apostles which he also ascribes to Luke. He owns likewise all the fourteen epistles of Paul except the epistle to Philemon. He has also quoted the first epistle of Peter, the 1st and 2d of John, Jude, and the Revelation."

After an examination of his citations from various Apocryphal works, he adds—"On the whole, it appears there is no good reason to suppose, that Clement received as Scripture in the highest sense of the word, *any* writings besides the books of the New Testament now commonly received by us." The remark is important; as Clemens is the only Father against whom the charge is made with any plausibility, of appealing to the authority of Apocryphal writers.

IRENÆUS, A. D. 170.

His testimony to the four Gospels is most explicit. "We have not received the knowledge of the way of our salvation by any others than those by whom the Gospel has been brought to us; which Gospel they first preached, and afterwards by the will of God committed to writing; that it might be for time to come the foundation and pillar of our faith. For after that our Lord rose from the dead, the apostles . . . received a perfect knowledge of all things. They then went forth to all the ends of the earth, declaring to men the blessing of heavenly peace, having all of them and every one alike, the Gospel of God. Matthew then, among the Jews, wrote a Gospel in their own language. Mark also, the disciple and interpreter of Peter, delivered to us in writing, things that had been preached by Peter; and Luke, the companion of Paul, put down in a book the Gospel preached by him [Paul]. Afterwards, John, the disciple of the Lord, who also leaned upon his breast, published a Gospel while he dwelt at Ephesus in Asia. And he who does not assent to them despiseth, indeed, those who knew the mind of the Lord: but he *despiseth also Christ himself* the Lord; and he despiseth likewise the Father, and is self-condemned, resisting and opposing his own salvation."

That he received all the epistles of Paul, is evinced by his numerous quotations from all of them except Philemon and the Hebrews, of which Dr. Lardner gives eighteen examples. "The same thing Paul has explained in the Romans:" "This, Paul manifestly shows in the epistle to the Corinthians:" "As the blessed Paul says in the epistle to the Ephesians," and other like expressions continually occur in his writings. The Revelation, he expressly ascribes to "John the disciple of Christ." Dr. Lardner says, his testimony is so strong and full, that he seems to put it beyond all question that it is the work of John the Apostle.

JUSTIN MARTYR, A. D. 130.

The writings of this eminent man, born not long after the death of the Apostles, and acquainted with their immediate disciples,—though few and small, are rich in references to the New Testament. He seldom names the particular books. But in these early times, there were no controversies rendering it necessary. He often speaks of the Gospels as "Memoirs of Christ," and says, that "the Apostles composed them." In his writings there are references more or less clear (Dr. L. gives fifteen) to Acts, Rom. Cor. Gal. Eph. Phil. Col. Thess. Heb. Peter and the Revelation, which last he expressly ascribes to the Apostle John.

He also declares it to be a general practice, that "the Gospels are read at public worship in Christian assemblies every Lord's day as the time allows, and when the reader has ended, the President makes a discourse exhorting to the imitation of so excellent things." This is a striking fact, proving that so early as the beginning of the second century, they were acknowledged to be genuine, regarded with the highest esteem, and open to all the world.

A similar testimony might have been quoted from Tertullian, "We come together, he says, "to recollect the Divine Scriptures. We nourish our faith, raise our hope, confirm our trust by the sacred word."

OLD TRANSLATIONS BETWEEN 100 AND 200.

It does not admit a doubt, that the old Syriac version, which has come down to us in a sound condition, was composed at this early period. The more ancient copies want 2d Peter, 2d and 3d John, and probably James: and this circumstance probably fostered the doubts of the early fathers concering these books. But with regard to all the others, it is complete. The old Italic versions for they were many, have also come down more or less perfect. They were composed at the same period; and the fact that Jerome, who in the fourth century digested them into one (the present Latin Vulgate) which contains precisely our books, says nothing of having added to the collection, proves satisfactorily that it was the same with his own.

I. CENTURY.

APOSTOLIC FATHERS.

We have now reached the age of the immediate disciples and contemporaries of the Apostles. If the evidence be not so full and overpowering as that of the following times, let it be considered—

1st. That exceedingly little remains of the genuine writings of the Apostolical Fathers. The whole can be contained in a pamphlet of thirty pages.

2d. What we have, is pious exhortation, that does not require appeals to authority.

3d. The various books had not yet been so extensively circulated, as to make it certain that every Christian church was acquainted with them. It required some time therefore, to *establish the custom* of quoting them.

POLYCARP, A. D. 100.

All that remains of this holy martyr, is a short letter to the Philippians, in which he distinctly refers to the *epistle of Paul to that church*—" For neither I nor any one like me, can come up to the wisdom of blessed and renowned Paul, who when absent, wrote to you (the Philippians) an epistle."

Occasionally he quotes passages with some formality, as—

NEW TESTAMENT.	POLYCARP.
1 Cor. vi. 2. Do ye not know that the saints shall judge the world?	"Do we not know that the saints shall judge the world?" as Paul teaches.
Eph. iv. 26. Be ye angry and sin not: let not the sun go down upon your wrath.	"For I trust that ye are well exercised in the holy scriptures: 'As in these scriptures it is said: Be ye angry and sin not. And let not the sun go down upon your wrath.'"
Matt. v. 3. Blessed are the poor in spirit: for theirs is the kingdom of heaven. 7. Blessed are the merciful, for they shall obtain mercy. Blessed are they which are persecuted for righteousness' sake, for theirs is the kingdom of heaven.	"But remembering what the Lord said: 'Be ye merciful, that ye may obtain mercy. Blessed are the poor, and they that are persecuted for righteousness sake: for theirs is the kingdom of God.'"
Luke vi. 37. Judge not, and ye shall not be judged.	"The Lord said, 'Judge not, that ye be not judged.'"
Mark xiv. 38. The spirit indeed is willing, but the flesh is weak.	"The Lord hath said, 'The spirit indeed is willing, but the flesh is weak."

More frequently, he only refers to passages; borrowing the sentiments and language of the sacred writers, without expressly naming them, as—

N. T.	POLYCARP.
Acts ii. 24. Whom God hath raised up, having loosed the pains of death.	"Whom God hath raised, having loosed the pains of hell."
Rom. xiv. 10. We shall all stand before the judgment seat of Christ. 12. So, then, every one of us shall give an account of himself to God.	"And must all stand before the judgment seat of Christ, and every one give an account for himself."
1 Cor. vi. 9. Neither fornicators, nor idolators, nor adulterers, nor effeminate, nor abusers of themselves with mankind; 10. Shall inherit the kingdom of God.	"And neither fornicators, nor effeminate, nor abusers of themselves with mankind, shall inherit the kingdom of God."
Eph. ii. 8. For by grace are ye saved through faith: and that not of yourselves: it is the gift of God—not of works.	"Knowing that by grace ye are saved not of works, but by the will of God through Jesus Christ."

1 Thess. v. 17. Pray without ceasing.	"Praying without ceasing for all."
1 Tim. vi. 7. For we brought nothing with us into this world, and it is certain we can carry nothing out. 10. For the love of money is the root of all evil.	"The love of money is the beginning of all troubles. Knowing, therefore, that as we brought nothing into the world, so neither can we carry anything out."
1 Pet. i. 8. Whom having not seen ye love; in whom though now ye see him not, yet believing ye rejoice with joy unspeakable and full of glory.	"In whom though ye see him not ye believe, and believing ye rejoice with joy unspeakable and full of glory."
1 Pet. ii. 22. Who did no sin, neither was guile found in his mouth. 23. Who his own self bare our sins in his own body on the tree.	"Who bare our sins in his own body on the tree; who did no sin, neither was guile found in his mouth."
1 John iv. 3. And every spirit, that confesseth not that Jesus Christ has come in the flesh, is not of God: and this is that spirit of Antichrist, whereof you have heard, &c.	"For whoever confesseth not that Jesus Christ is come in the flesh, is Antichrist."

Nearly thirty examples of this kind are found in this brief letter; proving the author's perfect familiarity with all the books of the New Testament, except a few of the minor epistles.

IGNATIUS, A. D. 100.

According to Chrysostom, he personally conversed with many of the Apostles. The only genuine remains of him are seven short epistles. One is a letter to the Ephesians, in which he expressly mentions *the epistle written to them* a few years before by Paul. "Ye are the companions (he says) in the mysteries of the Gospel of the blessed Paul, who throughout all his epistle makes mention of (i. e. commends) you in Christ Jesus."

This is the only book expressly named, but there are more than forty examples in the few pages which contain his writings, of his employing the language of the New Testament: with which he must therefore have been acquainted, as—

N. T.	IGNATIUS.
Matt. iii. 15. For thus it becomes us to fulfil all righteousness.	"Baptised of John, that all righteousness might be fulfilled by him."
Matt. x. 16. Be ye therefore wise as serpents, and harmless as doves.	"Be wise as a serpent in all things and harmless as a dove."

John iii. 8. The wind bloweth where it listeth, and thou hearest the sound thereof: but canst not tell whence it cometh and whither it goeth: so is every one that is born of the spirit.	"The spirit is not deceived, being from God: for it knows whence it comes, and whither it goes, and reproves secret things."
Acts x. 41. Who did eat and drink with him after he arose from the dead.	"But after his resurrection he did eat and drink with them.
1 Cor. i. 18. For the preaching of the cross is to them that perish foolishness: but unto us which are saved it is the power of God. 19. For it is written—I will bring to nothing the understanding of the prudent. 20. Where is the wise? Where is the scribe? Where is the disputer of this world?	"Let my life be sacrificed for the doctrine of the cross, which is a stumbling-block unto unbelievers, but to us salva. tion and life eternal. Where is the wise? Where is the disputer? Where is the boasting of them that are called prudent?
Eph. v. 25. Husbands love your wives, even as Christ also loved the Church and gave himself for it.	"Exhort my brethren, in the name of Jesus Christ, to love their wives as the Lord the Church."

The reference to other books, particularly Philippians, Colossians, Thessalonians, Timothy, Titus, 1st and 2d John, are equally striking and unequivocal.

CLEMENS ROMANUS, A. D. 96.

The friend and fellow-laborer of Paul, whom he specially names in Phil. iv. 3. So the ancients positively attest, without a dissenting voice. He has only left a short epistle to the Corinthians. In it, Paul's *epistle to the same church* is expressly mentioned.

N. T.	CLEMENS.
1 Cor. i. 11-12. For it hath been declared unto me of you, my brethren, . . . that there are contentions among you. Now this I say, that every one of you saith that I am of Paul; and I of Apollos; and I of Cephas; and I of Christ."	"Take into your hands the epistle of the blessed Paul the apostle. What did he at the first write to you in the beginning of the Gospel? Verily he did by the spirit admonish you concerning himself and Cephas and Apollos, because that even then, you did form parties.

This is the only instance of a book of the New Testament being named. But there are more than forty manifest references like the following:

N. T.	CLEMENS.
Matt. xxvi. 24. Woe to that man by whom the Son of Man is betrayed: it had been good for that man if he had not been born. Matt. xviii 6. Whoso shall offend one of these little ones which believe in me, it were better for him that a millstone were hanged about his neck and that he were drowned in the depth of the sea.	"Remember the words of the Lord Jesus. For he said, 'Woe to that man [by whom offences come.] It were better for him that he had not been born than that he should offend one of my elect. It were better for him that a millstone should be tied about his neck, and that he should be drowned in the sea, than that he should offend one of my little ones."
Luke vi. 36. Be ye therefore merciful as your Father also is merciful.	"Especially remembering the words of the Lord Jesus, 'Be ye merciful that ye may obtain mercy.'"
Rom. i. 29. Being filled with all unrighteousness, fornication, wickedness, covetousness, maliciousness; full of envy, murder, debate, deceit, malignity, whisperings, (30) backbiters, haters of God, despiteful, proud, boasters. 32. Who knowing the judgment of God (that they which do such things are worthy of death) not only do the same, but have pleasure in them that do them.	"Casting off from us all 'unrighteousness and iniquity, covetousness, debates, malignities, deceits, whisperings backbitings, hatred of God, pride, boasting,' and vainglory and ambition. 'For they that do these things are hateful to God: and not only they that do them, but they also who have pleasure in them."
1 Cor. 15-20. But now is Christ risen from the dead, and become the first fruits of them that slept.	"Let us consider, beloved, how the Lord does continually show us, that there shall be a resurrection. Of which he has made the Lord Jesus Christ the first fruits, having raised him from the dead."
1 Tim. ii. 8. I will therefore, that men pray everywhere, lifting up holy hands without wrath and doubting.	"Let us therefore come to him in holiness of soul, lifting up to him chaste and undefiled hands."
Eph. iv. 4. There is one body and one spirit, even as ye are called in one hope of your calling. 5. One Lord, one faith, one baptism. 6. One God and Father of all.	"Have we not one God, and one Christ? And is there not one spirit poured out upon us, and one calling in Christ."
Heb. iii. 5. And Moses verily was faithful in all his house.	"When also Moses, that blessed and 'faithful' servant in all his house."
1 Peter iv. 8. For charity shall cover a multitude of sins.	"Charity covers the multitude of sins."

2 Peter ii. 5. And saved Noah a preacher of righteousness.	Noah preached repentance, and they who hearkened [to him] were saved."

Such coincidences of thought and expression, it is impossible to consider as accidental. On the whole, it seems *certain*, that Clement had in his hands at least the first three Gospels, the Acts, and the five principal epistles of Paul.

SUMMARY.

As the mind is apt to be confused and lost in a multitude of quotations, we shall endeavor to aid the reader, by a brief commentary and summing up.

Commencing with the fourth century for a reason already given, we find that no less than *ten* principal writers have furnished catalogues, six of which, agree perfectly with our collection. The others, only differ in this; that they omit the Revelation, and one of them the epistle to the Hebrews. How perfectly decisive this fact!

Moving our post of observation to the third century, we do not find such a number of regular catalogues: indeed, there are but two that may be called complete. Yet the evidence is equally satisfying. The number of writers from whom Lardner quotes in proof of the existence and full of recognition of our books, is about *forty*, of whom it would be hardly too bold to say, that they are of "every nation, and kindred, and tongue and people." Even the dark forests of Germany, send forth a trumpet voice in attestation of the Christian verity. We refer to the venerable martyr

Victorinus, bishop of Pettaw, a town on the river Drave. He expressly quotes the four Gospels by name. He quotes also the Acts, and speaks of the seven churches to which Paul wrote epistles. "Afterwards (he adds) he wrote to particular persons; undoubtedly, he means, Timothy, Titus, and Philemon. On the Revelation, he wrote an elaborate commentary.

The works of Cyprian, bishop of Carthage, overflow with citations, except from James, Jude, 2d Peter, and the epistle to the Hebrews, to which no reference is made. The four Gospels, he mentions frequently. Every epistle of Paul is referred to, with the exception specified. So, are most of the Catholic epistles. Mark also the fact, that in that distinguished Bishop, there is not one quotation from any spurious or apocryphal writer.

Of the profound and critical Origen, Dr. Mill makes this striking remark: "Quotations of Scripture are so thickly sown, that if we had all his works remaining, we should have before us almost *the whole text of the Bible*." His catalogue has been given in our Synopsis. All necessary to be remembered in examining it, is the distinction made by Eusebius between the "controverted" (αντιλεγομενα) books, and those "universally acknowledged" (ωμολογουμενα) to which Origen subscribes.

Pursuing our course upward, we come to the second century; and the first whom we meet, is the eloquent

Tertullian, of whom Dr. Lardner observes: "there are in him more and larger quotations from the small volume of the New Testament, than there *are of all the works of Cicero, in writers of all characters for several ages.*" Of the Gospels, he says: "we lay this down for a certain truth, that the evangelic scriptures, have for their authors, men to whom the work of publishing the Gospel was committed by the Lord himself. Concerning the epistles of Paul, he says: "let us then see what milk the Corinthians received from Paul, to what rule the Galatians were subjected, what the Philippians read," &c. The only books not used by him, are James, 2d Peter, 2d and 3d John.

Equally ample is the testimony of Clement of Alexandria. He asserts in various places that there are four Gospels. He receives the Acts of the Apostles, and quotes frequently the various epistles of Paul.

The evidence of Irenæus, bishop of Lyons in France, is so exceedingly valuable, that we have quoted largely from him. We find, that he received the four Gospels, and thirteen epistles of Paul, which he expressly cites. No apocryphal book is mentioned by him, as having any authority.

We close the reviews of this century, with Justin Martyr; one of the many in these days, who died for their religion. The synopsis shows, that he frequently refers to our Gospels, though he does not name their authors, but calls them the "Memoirs of the Apostles." There are also distinct references to the Acts, the Epistles to the Corinthians, Colossians &c. Justin was born, according to some, in the year 89; some, place him a few years later. How decisive is this for the genuineness of our books! When we quoted the last two or three writers, we came within a generation of the very men, who are alleged without a dissenting voice to have written their records; and the light of tradition still beams forth radiant and clear. How *could* these people be deceived in a matter so interesting to the Christian as the writing of his sacred books—when their authors had not been dead forty years? The very *supposition makes them idiots.*

The *testimony that* follows of the *old Syriac* and Italic *versions, speaks* for itself, *and needs no comment.*

We come now, to the venerable men who lived in the times of tbe Apostles, and were honored with their immediate instructions; for which reason, they are usually called the "Apostolical Fathers." Though we are able to present few strongly marked and formal quotations, yet that they were acquainted with, many, if not all, our sacred books, is beyond a doubt. Let the reader examine our synopsis, marking the identity of thought and phrase between the extracts from them, and the passages of the New Testament in the opposite column, and he will find it impossible to adopt any other conclusion. Besides, there are express quotations by Barnabas, Clemens, Romanus,

Ignatius, and Polycarp, which we will not injure by an attempt at compression.

After all, we have confessed, that the evidence of these holy men is not so overpowering as that of their successors. But we have also explained it. Their works that remain, are very few and short: all that is authentic, could be printed on twenty octavo pages. The subjects on which they wrote, were simple and practical, not requiring an appeal to authorities. It must be remembered also, that the books of the New Testament had been freshly written, and not yet distributed through the churches, or collected into a canon. In quoting therefore largely from any of them, they ran some risk of not being understood. Strength is given to this supposition, by the fact, that when they knew from the circumstances of the case, that those whom they addressed were acquainted with a particular writing, they actually used it. Thus Clemens, writing to the Corinthians, quotes Paul's epistle to that church; and Barnabas, writing to the Philippians, mentions his epistle to *them*.

We here close the argument. Brief and imperfect as the statement has been, we fear that some will find it disagreeably long. But we cannot, (and we would not, if we could,) turn an inquiry of this kind into an Arabian tale. What is said of gold, that the richest mines are often found in the most arid and inhospitable regions, may be applied to truth. Its most valuable treasures frequently lie concealed in the most dry and uninteresting discussions; and doubtless this is the reason, why they are so rarely discovered.

NATURE OF THE EVIDENCE.

Before leaving the subject, we shall make a reflection on the nature of the evidence adduced. It claims no mysterious sanctity, but is simply *historical*—being the very same that is applied to the genuineness of any other production. Why do we receive the Commentaries of Cæsar, and the Annals of Tacitus, as the works of these eminent men? Because their authorship is asserted by the general voice of antiquity. They are quoted as the authors, by writers, who, from their honesty, research, and proximity to the time in which they lived, were fully qualified to pronounce judgment. They are cited by enemies, and proofs of genuineness are found in every page of the writings themselves. We all understand such appeals. There is a natural logic in the breast of almost every man, which seldom fails of leading to the right conclusion. It is true, that the evidence is not in the strict sense of the word, (in the mathematician's sense), demonstrative: but it is the same that guides us in all matters of fact, and common life. How do we know the truth of any thing that is narrated to us, which we did not observe personally?

Why do we believe that there was an ancient city called Nineveh, or that the English John signed the Magna Charta? Can they be proved by diagrams—or evolved from an equation? Can it be shown, that their denial contradicts some necessary or immutable truth? Yet who refuses to admit them; and what name would we give a man, who, because their evidence belongs to the kind which logicians call *probability*, plays the sceptic, but that of a fool, better qualified for Bedlam, than to converse with his fellow men?

. . . To all this, we assent without difficulty, some may reply. We are quite ready to believe without Euclid, that Thucydides wrote the history of the Peloponnesian war, and Cicero the orations against Verres. But when works offer themselves to our attention and claim our regard, as productions of men *divinely inspired*, a much heavier draft is made on the bank of faith. Far weightier proof is necessary, to establish the origination of miraculous narratives from the men who professed to have seen the facts, than to prove that a relation of probable, every-day occurrences, is truly his, whose name it bears. We concede the perfect fairness of this demand; provided the evidence required, is only greater in *degree*—not different in kind. God *might* have made the proofs of our religion, more overpowering than the evidence of mathematics itself: he might have uttered them in thunder; and written them with a pen of fire in the skies. But he has not adopted this course; as he designed our present state to be imperfect and probationary, in which our faculties should be called forth by the powerful stimulus of necessity, our principles tried, and the moral character formed for eternity. Now, these results could not be attained, by placing us in the noon-tide light which many thoughtlessly desire. Faith would cease to be a virtue, in a world so constituted: Holiness would become a service of compulsion, and man a slave. Meanwhile, if we see here "through a glass," darkly, it is our comfort to know, that we have light enough to direct us, if we faithfully improve it. "Men have reason," says the sagacious Locke, "to be well satisfied with what God has done for them; since he has given whatever is necessary for convenience of life and information of virtue; and has put within their reach if they are willing to make search, to which, however, he will not compel them, a comfortable provision for this life, and the way that leads to a better. We shall not have much need to complain of the narrowness of our minds, if we will employ them about what may be of use to us; and it will be an unpardonable as well as childish peevishness, if we undervalue the advantages of our knowledge, and neglect to improve it, because there are some things that are set out of its reach."

With regard to the subject discussed, our brief examination shows with what little reason, want of evidence can be alleged. It is indeed of the same kind with that of productions merely human. But in degree it is far more ample and satisfying, than all that has ever been advanced for any book of equal antiquity.

CHAPTER II.

CANON OF THE OLD TESTAMENT.

§ 1.—*The Proof.*

We propose to arrive at our conclusion on this important subject, by a shorter route than that which is frequently adopted. The Old Testament, in regard both to its genuineness and canonical authority, shall be built upon the New; and as believers in the Son of God, we feel certain that it is a foundation strong enough to sustain the whole edifice.

It is not said, that this volume possesses no independent evidence—that no appeal can be made to national tradition; to the scrupulous care with which the Jews guarded their sacred writings; to the support these writings receive from the traditions of other nations; and to their internal marks of genuineness. It does not hang thus in the air. But this *is* asserted, that a man of fair mind, whose faculties have been sharpened by habits of critical analysis, cannot retire from such an investigation, without a feeling of doubt and disappointment. The main argument, that from national tradition, is much more plausible than solid. During the last two thousand years, indeed, the Jews have exhibited the most intense devotion to their sacred books: it has been, and still is their ruling passion, sometimes even rising to maniacal excitement, as could easily be shown from their history. This, combined with the fact, that during almost the whole of the period mentioned, they have possessed a regular body of learned men, who watch over the purity of their volume, is a good argument for its existence and preservation, since the fourth or fifth century preceding the birth of Christ. But the philosophical inquirer will remind us, that this has not *always* been the case. The ruling passion, in nations as in men, is subject to change, and the change is so astonishing oftentimes, that the subjects of it hardly retain a single feature of character, by which they can be identified with what they were. What a contrast between the old Roman, and his modern descendants; between the Mexican, and the Castilian, of the fifteenth century! That a revolution equally great has been experienced by the Jews, is beyond dispute. Let the single example suffice, of their return during their captivity in Babylon to the doctrine of the Divine Unity, which they have maintained ever since, with a fidelity truly admirable, when before that time, their love of idolatry was a perfect madness. Nor is it possible to disguise another fact bearing yet more directly on the subject—that from the reign of Solomon, to the dethronement of their last king by Nebuchadnezzar, they evinced the most stupid indifference to their religious writings as well as institutions. Forgeries, therefore, might easily have taken place.

If the small literary coterie, to whom the people blindly submitted in every thing pertaining to learning and religion, chose to impose upon them certain myths, fragments of song, and annals of olden time, as the "sacred library," which had come down from their remote ancestors, there was positively nothing in the character of the nation to prevent it.

This is only a specimen of the numerous doubts that will disturb the most honest mind, in view of the difficulties connected with an independent demonstration of the canonical authority of the Old Testament. Let us be thankful that we are not compelled to the arduous task of encountering them; and that we have a ground of certainty, from which no array of learning or ingenuity can dislodge us. Let us accept with gratitude, the authoritative dicta of the divine Founder of Christianity, and not blush to acknowledge that our Bible, our whole Bible, comes from his sacred hand!

With this infallible guidance, the enlightened Christian feels perfectly safe. In the many questions raised by unbelievers, concerning the possibility of introducing spurious writings before the advent of the great teacher, he may take a strong literary and historical, but not a great religious interest. Their "Pseudo Isaiahs," and "Pseudo Daniels," will not disconcert him in the least. Their positions he believes to be false, and incapable of being substantiated by fair argument: but even though he could not prove their fallacy by positive demonstration, he has all that is needed, in the "*imprimatur*" of one who never deceived him, and on whose perfect truth he has staked his immortality. The man who has *given his soul to Christ*, can have no scruple to trust him with settling his rule of faith.

OUR COLLECTION APPROVED BY CHRIST. TWO METHODS OF PROOF.

What, then, is the testimony of our Redeemer and his inspired apostles, regarding our volume? Though they have nowhere given a formal catalogue, ample information can be obtained from them in two different ways:

1st. By ascertaining what books they quote, or directly refer to:

2dly. By inquiring what was the established Canon of the Jews, at the time they lived; and whether there is evidence that they adopted it.

FIRST METHOD: DIRECT QUOTATIONS.

1st. This point shall detain us but a moment. The highly satisfactory statement can be made at once, that there are in the New Testament *distinct references to all the books of the Old*—(to Genesis, Exodus, &c., &c.,) except Ruth, Ezra, Esther, Ecclesiastes, Song of Solomon. The seal of the author of

Christianity is thus stamped upon our whole collection, with the exception of four or five books; and the silence concerning these is perfectly natural. There was no occasion of appealing to them: indeed, the wonder is, that so small a book as the New Testament should be found to have honored its elder sister with so *many* notices, (256 direct citations, and 283 references), not that a few of its smaller portions should be passed over. Equally striking is the fact, that with one or two exceptions, more apparent than real, no notice is taken of any Apocryphal books. Whenever a quotation is made, we know at once where to find it in the Old Volume. Cruden's Concordance will direct to the book, the chapter, and the verse. Such are the results to which we are led by the *first* method. Supposing our volume to consist of five hundred pages, we may say that four hundred and ninety bear the legible signature of the incarnate "wisdom of God."

SECOND METHOD: CHRIST ADOPTED THE ESTABLISHED CANON OF HIS COUNTRYMEN.

After all, the evidence is not perfect. Some books, as we have observed, are passed over. Is it not possible then, to settle the question with a little more precision? We answer, by calling the reader's attention to the 2d method—that of ascertaining *whether the Jews had an established and universally recognized collection, at the time of our Lord's appearing, and whether there is good reason to believe that he adopted it.*

On the latter point, which it is convenient to dispose of first, one answer only can be given. Whatever the Jewish collection was, Jesus Christ most certainly approved it. We repeat the assertion, and with emphasis: Whatever the Jewish collection was—*Jesus Christ most certainly approved it.* He did so, by his uniform practice of appealing to the same books which they made use of, and attributing to them the same Divine authority, without ever hinting that there was the least discrepancy between their views and his own. None can charge him with want of moral courage in administering reproof. How often did the corrupt Pharisees writhe under the lash of his cutting denunciations! Their hypocrisy and pride, their savage cruelty, their lust for power and riches, their compassing sea and land to make one proselyte, who became in their hands more a child of hell than before, all these and other abominable traits of character, are painted as with a pencil dipt in fire; so that while reading his discourses, we cease to wonder at that demoniac fury, which cried in the ears of the Roman Governor, "Not this man, but Barabbas; Crucify him, Crucify him." Now, is it likely that this terrible reprover was all the while conniving at a crime, towering above every other, because more fatal in its consequences—the crime of adulterating the pure fountain of Divine truth? If the Jews had admitted any spurious or apocryphal books, would he not have upbraided them with it, and commanded his apostles to rectify the abuse? But not a hint of this kind is dropped. On the subject of the sacred books, both he and his disciples are as perfect Jews as ever trod the floor of a Synagogue. "Search your Scriptures," was his habitual language, "for these are they which testify of me." If, after this, Christ did not unqualifiedly accept the canon of his countrymen, the conclusion is unavoidable: he was an arch hypocrite and an impostor!

THE JEWISH CANON AGREES WITH OUR OWN.

But what was it? And where shall we find it? The goodness of Divine Providence, which has never ceased to watch over the Church, enables us to give a solid answer to these questions. We have the testimony of learned, honest, and every way qualified witnesses, from the times of our Lord himself, that a collection existed, and that it was the same with that which we hold in our hands.

TESTIMONY OF JOSEPHUS. BORN A. D. 37.

Let us hear, in the first place, the great historian of the Jewish nation. No man could be more favorably situated for knowing the truth. He was born about the time when our Redeemer died, and was therefore a contemporary of the Apostles. He was a priest, and must have been perfectly at home in the Ecclesiastics of that age; not to mention that he had constant access to the temple, where an authentic copy of the Scriptures was deposited.. His statement is the following:

"We have not among us innumerable books which contradict each other; but only *twenty-two* which contain the history of all past time, and are justly held to be divine. Five of these are from Moses; they contain laws and accounts of the human race, from its creation till the time of his death, comprehending a period of three thousand years. From the death of Moses to Artaxerxes, who after Xerxes reigned over the Persians, the prophets who lived after Moses have related, in thirteen books, what happened in their time. The other four books contain hymns to God, and rules of life to men. Since Artaxerxes, up to our time, every thing has been recorded; but these writings are not considered *so worthy of credit* as those written earlier, (i. e. before the time of Artaxerxes), because after that time there was no regular succession of prophets. What faith we attribute to our Scriptures, is manifest in our conduct. For it is innate with all Jews, to hold these books to be the word of God, and to firmly stand by them, nay die, if necessary, in their defence."

It is to be regretted, that in this remarkable passage he does not enumerate the books more particularly. But we know perfectly what the number "twenty-two" included. It was an arrangement universally adopted; and from the Talmud and early Christian writings, we discover that it comprised all the writings of our present canon. Besides, he in his writings, actually quotes from them all, excepting Proverbs, Ecclesiastes, Song of Solomon, and Job. Mark also, the judgment he pronounces on the Hellenistic or Hebrew Greek compositions, which are now known by the name of "Apocrypha;" for to them he undoubtedly refers, as they were all, by the acknowledgment of their warmest friends, written after the time of Artaxerxes. "They are not of equal authority with those before them."

PHILO, A.D. 41. ALSO CONTEMPORARY WITH THE APOSTLES.

Happily, we have another Jewish witness, who lived at the same time. Philo resided in Alexandria, the metropolis of Egypt. His testimony is most decided, in favor of our present canon. He does not indeed give a formal catalogue, but throws out in passing, observations which clearly show his opinion. The only books of which he makes no use, are Ruth, Nehemiah, Chronicles, Esther, and Lamentations.

That he was acquainted with the Apocryphal books, Ecclesiasticus, Baruch, Tobit, &c. &c., is certain; for he borrows phrases from them. But not in a single instance does he use them as authority, or even quote them. This fact speaks volumes. That he should be acquainted with these writings, and yet studiously avoid appealing to them, when he wishes to establish his opinions,—while abounding in quotations from the others, is perfectly inexplicable on every other supposition but one; viz., that he did not rank them among the Scriptures which his nation regarded as holy, and divine.

MELITO, FLOURISHED CENTURY II.

The next witness we cite, is a venerable Christian Bishop, who lived fifty or sixty years after the Apostles; and travelled into the East, for the express purpose of ascertaining from the Jews themselves, the contents, and number, of their sacred books. He thus states the result.

"Melito to his brother Onesimus, greeting: Whereas from your great earnestness for the Word, you have often wished to have selections from the law and the prophets, which relate to our faith, and to have an accurate account of the ancient books, how many they are in number, and what is their order: I have endeavored to effect this. As I was journeying in the East, I came to the place where these things were clearly exhibited, (probably one of the Jewish Colleges of theology), accurately ascertained the books of the Old Testament, and send you a catalogue. They are called as follows, Genesis, Exodus, Leviticus, &c. &c. The catalogue need not be given, as it is precisely the same with our own, excepting, that the two smallest portions, Nehemiah and Esther are included in Ezra, to which they stand closely related in their subject matter. *Not one Apocryphal book is named.*

THE TALMUD, CENTURY III.

This great body of Jewish traditional law, which represents the opinions of the nation at the time of its composition, and many ages previous, gives a full list of the canonical writings. After dividing them into three general classes, viz., "the Law—the Prophets—and the Chetubim or Miscellaneous books," it proceeds to name each, separately: and the list is precisely that contained in the first page of our Bibles. *It contains not a trace of any Apocryphal writing.*

CONCLUSION.

We might go on, and cite the enumerations of Origen, Jerome, Athanasius, Cyril, and others, living within the first four centuries. But it would be a wearisome repetition; for with the exception of one careless blunder of Origen, they are the very same, and agree with our own. They all reject the Apocryphal books, which Jerome expressly names, for the purpose of excluding them. "Every one but these (he says, referring to his catalogue) is to be placed among the Apocrypha." Therefore, the "Wisdom of Solomon" as it is called, "The book of Jesus, the son of Sirach, and Judith, and Tobit, *are not in the Canon.*"

We close with saying, that if any truth can be established by evidence, it is, that during three hundred years subsequent to the birth of Christ, our Old Testament, as at present acknowledged by all except the church of Rome, was universally recognized, to be a true and perfect collection of the divine writings of the ancient œconomy. The evidence possesses a completeness, of which not many historical facts so far removed from us in time, can boast. It is proved also by arguments which cannot be resisted or evaded, that Christ and his Apostles, endorsed this collection—adopting it, without addition or alteration. Two of their contempories, Jews by birth and religion, tell us, what it was, and their testimony is sustained in every part, by a succession of pious and learned men, from the first century to the fourth. If any man can still harbor a suspicion, that the Bible of our Redeemer, is not the Bible in present use by Protestant churches not only in our own land but throughout the world, let him play the Sceptic on all matters, which do not come under his personal observation.

APOCRYPHA.

In adducing the preceding testimony,—frequent reference has been made, to certain books, for which a claim has been set up by the Catholic church, but which, for good reasons, Protestants have branded with the name "Apocryphal." They are ten in number ; viz., Baruch, Ecclesiasticus, Wisdom of Solomon,

Tobit, Judith, the two books of Maccabees, Additions to Esther, Song of the three Children, Susannah, Bell and the Dragon. The utter vanity of their pretentions has been shown by the entire silence of Christ and his Apostles—by the silence of Josephus, Philo, and the Talmud—and by their exclusion from the catalogues of all the Christian fathers, of the first four centuries. All this, seems perfectly clear and decisive. Yet the question will naturally occur to the student, how, under these circumstances, they obtained such currency among Christians, as to make any claim *at all!* We shall answer this inquiry, by giving, in a few words, their history.

As to the time in which they were written, there is proof on every page, that they belong to the latter age of Jewish literature, which commenced a little after the time of Alexander the Great, about three hundred years before the advent of our Lord. In consequence of various favorable circumstances, a new impulse was given at this period to Hebrew genius; and many respectable efforts were made by it, in different kinds of composition. The language employed, was—in Palestine, the Chaldaic dialect: but the principal seat of this literary revival, was Alexandria, in Egypt. In that immense city, the Jews were so numerous, that according to some historians, they constituted nearly half of the whole population. All these, spoke the Greek language, and adopted to some extent the Greek manners, from which circumstance, they received the name of "Hellenists," or *Grecizers.* Having become somewhat refined by constant intercourse with their polished neighbors, they contracted, as has been already stated, a fondness for books, and writers soon appeared to gratify their taste.

Such was the origin of the "Apocrypha." It is nothing more or less, than the remains of that Hellenistic or Jewish Greek literature, which flourished in Alexandria, within the period of three hundred years before the birth of Christ. There is not the least reason to believe, that the Jews thought of comparing them to Canonical Scriptures. This blunder, was committed by *Christians*, and it took place in the following manner. In the third century before Christ, some learned men favored their countrymen in Alexandria, with a Greek translation of the Old Testament, which, from the supposed number of its authors, was called the "Septuagint," or Version of the Seventy. It was cordially welcomed: Every Jew would have a copy, and for convenience sake, he would attach to it the writings of which we are giving an account, that he might have a complete religious library in one roll or volume. The practice was not without its advantages; and in the case of the Jews themselves, who well knew their canon, was followed by no bad consequences. But when the Septuagint, thus crammed with foreign matter, came into the hands of Christians, the important distinction between divine and human productions, was often overlooked:

as it might be with us, if the custom prevailed of binding up old Bunyan's "Pilgrim," or any other such pious composition with the sacred volume. We need not be surprised therefore, if even a good Christian Bishop, is sometimes found nodding,—and quoting his Bunyan, instead of his Bible.

In this state, things remained, until the middle of the fourth century; the catalogues and learned opinion being always right; while the practice was occasionally loose, and wrong. At this time, the first symptom appears of a disposition to give them a place in the Canon; which was actually done in the Council of Carthage, A. D. 397. After this, they met with general acceptance; which however will excite no surprise in those who are acquainted with ecclesiastical history. In other respects beside the corruption of her rule of faith, was that epoch the beginning of sorrows to the Church.

Nothing occurs, worthy of notice concerning them, until the Reformation. We may well suppose, that the men who led the vanguard of the great army of witnesses for the truth, would inquire with no little anxiety, into the purity of its fountains; and the result was what might have been expected. They discarded the Apocrypha, and returned to the good old Jewish canon of Christ and his Apostles.

§ 2.—*The Religious Value of the Old Testament.*

We propose to offer a few considerations on the value of the Old Testament, as part of our Christian rule of faith. There are many who do not scruple to express themselves on this point, in language bordering on profaneness; depriving it almost of every claim to our respect, except as a venerable reminiscence of antiquity. Even among persons who consider themselves decidedly evangelical, a doubt is often felt, whether it has not been entirely superceded by the more brilliant light of Christianity—and whether any great injury would be sustained, if, while it continued to be employed as a reading-book in the instruction of youth, it ceased to exert authority over the conscience: a few reflections, therefore, on the unspeakable value and importance of our volume, will not be out of place.

In discussing this point, we do not feel called to institute any invidious comparisons between the Old Testament and the New. Rivalry can have no place between two œconomies, which differ only as to the degree of light, in which the same blessed plan of saving mercy has been presented to mankind: they form one great system, and their respective books are in the most perfect and lovely harmony with each other. As the Old Testament cannot say to the New, "I have no need of thee;" so the New cannot say to the Old, "I have no need of thee." Will it be objected that the worth and necessity of the elder revelation are impaired by the fact, that whatever it contains of primary importance is repeated in the younger? We deny the assertion: it does not repeat the instructions of its predecessor, but *assumes* them. It addresses us as if they were our old and familiar acquaintances; and proceeds to build on the already half-built edifice, what is peculiarly its own. Perhaps the proposition we are about enouncing may sound much like paradox: but we are certain of its truth. It is, that the New Testament, without the Old, is as imperfect a revelation as the Old without the New. What immense masses of instruction, the most interesting and precious, are contained in the former, without a knowledge of which it is impossible to understand the latter; and yet which the latter scarcely touches, or treats only in the way of hint and allusion! This thought deserves a full illustration.

DEPENDENCE OF THE NEW TESTAMENT ON THE OLD.

The fundamental doctrine of the Divine Unity and Spirituality, is a truth which faith receives, on the authority of our volume: in the New, it is rarely stated, though of course, always recognized as the main pillar of true religion. Why should we wonder at its dearth of assertion, when the most ample information was already imparted to the world? "Hear, O Israel, the Lord thy God is one Jehovah," forms the central truth of the ancient œconomy, the maintenance of which, against a universal deluge of superstition and idolatry, is represented to be one principal design of God's separating to himself a peculiar people. Wonderful, indeed it must appear, that a theology so beautiful and pure, so sublime, and agreeable to all the principles of reason, as that which adopts as its corner stone the divine unity and immateriality, should have vanished from the minds of men, and given place to a foul and corrupting polytheism! But such was the fact. Let us adore the goodness of God in providing a remedy, by lighting up at so early a period the lamp of truth on the sacred hills of Palestine, where it shone with unceasing radiance, and gradually enlarged its horizon, until it was lost in the more dazzling splendor of the sun of righteousness.

To the same source we must betake for authentic information concerning the creation and origin of all things: here, also, the New Testament points back to its predecessor, and commits us to its infallible guidance. The light of nature, indeed, when uncorrupted, is able to teach us that the fair variety of things around us did not exist from eternity, but had a beginning. It suggests, however, only the fact. On the mode, time, order, with all the other circumstances which are necessary to make it strike the imagination and the heart, reason in the maturity of her powers maintains a sullen silence. But in the midst of the general darkness which followed the apostacy, even the *fact* was forgotten: the Gentile world knew as little of the creative power of God, as his unity and spirituality. The vulgar, blinded by their poets, thought that the world was eternal, or the work of chance; The philosopher either acquiesced in the absurdity, or heating his brain with fantastic speculations, gave birth to absurdities yet more monstrous. It was necessary therefore, that a voice should come forth from the heavenly sanctuary, to teach us that "the things which are seen, were not made of things that do appear." In the cosmogony of Moses, we have every thing which a reasonable curiosity could desire on this great subject; and the knowledge is communicated in such a manner as to purify the heart, and call into action its best affections. Who can read the first two chapters of Genesis without prostrating himself before that great being, "who spoke and it was done, commanded and it stood fast:" and when he reads of the ample provision made for the happiness of his creatures, who can forbear exclaiming, "O Lord, how manifold are thy works; in wisdom hast thou made them all; the earth is full of thy riches."

In the next place, our volume satisfies all reasonable inquiries concerning the original condition of man—inquiries which are not formally answered in the New Testament, for this plain reason, that the need of it is superceded by earlier revelations. On this, as on the two former topics, reason unassisted by faith is dumb. There seem, indeed, to have survived in the human mind some faint recollections of a happier state of things than the present, of which the heathen poets made a charming use, in their representations of a golden age: but these were dreams—fascinating to the imagination, rejected by the understanding as baseless chimeras. No man could believe on the testimony of professed dealers in fiction, a hypothesis so entirely at war with our actual condition; and accordingly we find, that the most grovelling ideas concerning the original state of human nature prevailed among the heathen. Man was the child of fate, or accident, or of some capricious being a little superior to himself; who moulded a lump of clay, and quickened it by fire stolen from heaven. His soul was a finer matter; and after a few years, both it and its grosser vehicle must return to earth, and be dissolved into their original elements.

How different from such base-born, brutalizing speculations, the authentic notices of our sacred volume! Man is the immediate work of that all-wise and almighty Being, who gives life and happiness to every thing that lives! He was formed in his own image—spiritual—intelligent—immortal. A high and glorious destiny was set before him; and meanwhile, until the prize should be won, he was enthroned vicarious monarch of creation in that magnificent grant: "Let him have dominion over fish of the sea, and fowl of the air, and every living thing, that moveth on the face of the earth." Such was human nature, when it first appeared among the sons of God!

Blessed be his name for a volume, which rescues us so completely from all belittling views of our original character—from the self-contempt, which observation of the present state of things is apt to engender! It reconciles man to himself, and enables him to rejoice *that he is a man!*

In the next place, it accounts for the origin of evil, and the existence of depravity. No problem has engaged so much the attention of inquiring men as this, and none has been found so difficult to solve. A score of theories might be mentioned; but they are all equally unsatisfactory. Nothing has ever been suggested by human wit, which can for a moment stand in comparison with the account of our venerable Scripture—an account so perfectly rational, that the keenest intellect finds nothing to object, and so admirably perspicuous, that a child can comprehend it. Man was originally holy, and happy, with every bias in favor of moral rectitude; but yet, for wise purposes, left to the freedom of his own will! He was fully able to stand; yet liable to fall! Tempted by a being of superior order, he yielded to animal appetite, and all that train of evils succeeded, by natural and just consequence, which we now deplore! We do not say that this solution removes all the metaphysical difficulties which attend the question of the origin of evil; but it is perfectly satisfactory, as far as it goes; while it administers the most instructive and solemn lessons!

What an affecting representation also does our volume give of the extent of human depravity! That the doctrine referred to is contained in the New Testament, cannot be doubted: but the Old is the proper fountain of both proof and illustration. Here, it is stated with an energy of expression, which must impress every serious mind: here too, it is proved by the most convincing of all arguments—history, and facts. What a shocking array of crime, and calamities the fruit of crime, passes before us, when we follow the sacred narrative from its opening scene to the Babylonian captivity! How soon did violence fill the earth; and iniquity become so rampant, that it could only be removed by an universal deluge! After the flood, how soon did it reappear, so that God was prevented from inflicting a second catastrophe only by the promise, that he would not again curse the earth for man's sake. But it is needless to enlarge: every page is a commentary written in tears and blood, on its own declaration, that "the heart is deceitful above all things, and desperately wicked." Some have complained, that the Old Testament should abound in so many tragic and revolting details: but they forget that the history of our race could not be otherwise. What is man, but that very being whom the Bible describes? It is a faithful mirror, in which we see our own character: if the image be foul, let us attribute it to the true cause; and betake to the cleansing fountain of divine grace.

The doctrine of vicarious atonement is another of the great truths contained in our volume—which the New Testament assumes, rather than teaches. It everywhere, indeed, represents the Son of God as dying in the character of a substitute for the guilty; but in such a way, as to indicate that its reader is already familiar with the idea. Take away from Scripture that portion which teaches the origin of sacrifices, and the institution of them as the basis of all acceptable worship to God, we do not hesitate to say, that you inflict on the doctrine of salvation by the Redeemer's blood, a mortal wound. The modern adversaries of the truth feel this. They perceive that the doctrine of vicarious suffering, pervades the Old Testament, from Genesis to Malachi; that to deny it is mockery and folly: and their only resource is, to decry these precious records, as crammed with Jewish fable and superstition: a precious confession, that to get rid of atonement, they must join hands with the open infidel.

Equally valuable are its teachings, respecting the vital doctrine of our dependance on the Holy Spirit. No truth is more prominently held forth in the sublime theology of the Hebrews than this. In it, God is all in all: he not only moves amidst the scenes of external nature, riding on the whirlwind, sending down his rain and fruitful seasons, and causing the grass to grow for the service of man; but he is ever present with the souls that he has made. The hearts of men are represented as being in his hand, and he directs them like rivers of water. All excellent endowments of mind, all aspirations after the fair and good, all eminence in wisdom, political virtue and even secular art, are ascribed to the operation of the ever-acting, all-pervading *Ruah Jehova!* When we open the New Testament, therefore, we are fully prepared for the same great truth: we are not surprised to hear that every good and perfect gift cometh down from the Father of lights: we are not surprised at being told, that "unless a man be born of water and the Spirit, he cannot enter the kingdom of God:" nor to find the great Apostle of the Gentiles "bowing his knees before the Father of our Lord Jesus Christ, that he would grant us according to the riches of his glory, to be strengthened with might, by his spirit, in the inner man." What a comment on the Master's declaration, that "he came not to destroy the law and the prophets—that he came not to destroy, but to fulfil!" With what exquisite emotions must the pious Jew have discovered, that he "in whose lips grace was poured," but whom he had suspected of a design to overturn the faith of patriarchs and prophets, proffered to his acceptance the same *old religion* so dear to his heart, only purged from its defects, and expanded into the perfection of beauty! Such, we may suppose, was the state of mind expressed by Andrew, when he shouted that memorable declaration to his brother, Simon Peter, "We have found the Messias."

The discovery merited a shout: it was a ευρηκα, compared with which, that of the illustrious Sicilian sage was but an infant's babble: ευρηκαμεν τον χριστον; "WE HAVE FOUND—THE CHRIST!"

OLD TESTAMENT PIETY.

But a question here suggests itself, which even to well disposed and candid minds seems not a little perplexing. If the Old Testament be so rich in the vital and fundamental truths of our religion, how can the fact be explained, that the writers of the New Testament always represent the Mosaic institute to be a *hard and burdensome service*, which the people were scarcely able to bear? It consisted in bloody sacrifices, oblations, and complicated external observances, which "could not make him that did the service, perfect, as pertaining to the conscience;" and the writer to the Hebrews distinctly informs us that it was abrogated on account of its "weakness and unprofitableness." As much of the prejudice concerning our volume to which allusion has been made, is based on this view of the subject, we shall bestow on it a few remarks.

The whole difficulty originates in a gross misconception of the nature of the ancient œconomy. That the system which Moses by divine direction imposed upon the people, for special and temporary ends, had the character just described, is true—and that the piety which this system, left to its native workings, would generate, is very different from that produced by the operation of a pure Christianity, is equally so: but they who think that the members of the old Mosaic theocracy were restricted to the former, look only on the surface of things. They forget, or do not understand, that long before the civil and ecclesiastical organization by Moses, they had been placed under *another* dispensation of a very different nature —that of faith, of humble trust in the forgiving mercy of God, evincing itself by love, self-consecration, and holy obedience. The promise given to their father, Abraham, had a double aspect. It pledged the divine veracity, that a numerous posterity should issue from him, who should possess the land of Canaan: but beside this, was the promise of higher blessings, and a more glorious seed; through whom they should be secured, not only to him personally, but to all of every nation who would be partakers of his faith. This constitution, the Apostle, in Galatians iii. 17, tells us, "the law which was four hundred years after, could not annul nor contravene, so as to render the promise of no effect." Here—was the religion, under whose purifying influences that holy man "walked, as seeing him who is invisible, kept himself unspotted from the world, confessed himself a pilgrim and a stranger, and looked for a city that has foundations." This—was the religion, too, of all those noble spirits, of whom we have so glowing a description in the eleventh chapter of the Hebrews—of Isaac, of Jacob, of Joseph, of Moses, of Gideon, of Samuel and the prophets; who, "through faith subdued kingdoms, wrought righteousness, obtained promises, of whom the world was not worthy."

If we want to know the name and nature of this religion more definitely, the Apostle in his epistles to the Romans and Galatians, furnishes an answer. It was the religion of the *Gospel*—it was a *Christianity before Christ*—differing in none of its essential principles from that which we enjoy, being characterized as already said by the same reliance on the grace of a pardoning God—the same peace of conscience—the same fruits of holiness—and hope of immortality. The law of commandments contained in ordinances, with its ritual observances, and temporal retributions, was a constitution *superinduced* for certain special purposes—but did not supercede, nor abrogate it: like two parallel lines, they ran together through the whole œconomy; never interfering with or jostling each other; and yet so near, that the pious servant of God could enjoy the advantages of both, while the earthly mind saw only the earthly. As an Israelite of the natural stock of Abraham—in other words, as a member of the visible theocracy, he had his duties to perform—and *did* perform them. He walked in all the commandments and ordinances of the Lord blameless, performed his ablutions at the proper time and place, was ready on every proper occasion, with his sin, trespass, and burnt-offering, paid his tithes to the last farthing, gazed reverently at the nation's pontiff, while presiding over the nation's forms of worship—yet as a *man*, a partaker of Abraham's faith and exalted hopes of a spiritual redemption, he knew that he had "a more excellent way;" and gladly retired from the garish scene to some lonely spot, where undisturbed by the lowing of cattle, or the clash of sacrificial knives, he could pour out his soul to Abraham's God; the God, who not on this mountain nor on that—but everywhere, through the great cathedral of his universe, is worshipped by the pure spirit! Hence the observation of our pious Puritan divines, that believers of the old covenant lived *under* the law, but did not live *upon* the law. We mistake the matter entirely, when in trying to form a distinct conception of the religion of God's ancient church, we call up the temple, with its marble courts, its stately porticoes, and thousand priests standing in robes of white round the brazen altar and molten sea. The search must be made in quite another direction. We must visit the private dwelling—steal, if possible, into the sacred υπεϱωιον, or chamber of retirement on the house-top, where David panted as the "hart after the water-brooks," where Daniel "sought the Lord by prayer and supplication with sackcloth and ashes," where Isaiah mingled with the seraphim before the great "high throne"—or we must get to the top of Horeb, where Elijah talked mournfully with God over the abounding wickedness of his people!

In perfect agreement with this, is a fact which cannot escape the careful reader of the Old Testament, and is an extremely interesting one; viz. that in all those portions which exhibit the interior religious life of the people, there is scarcely an allusion to levitical peculiarities: it would seem, that the moment a pious soul felt itself alone with God, it shook off everything low and terrestrial which belonged to that dispensation of forms, forgot even the Jehova between the Cherubim, and soared away to the presence chamber of the upper sanctuary. Look through the Psalms—those wonderful compositions, which the infidel himself, if possessing one grain of taste or moral discernment, can never cease admiring for the rational and enlightened views, as well as pure seraphic devotion that breathe in every line: is it speaking too strongly to say, that did we not know from other sources the existence of a complicated ritual system among the people by whom they were sung, we would not believe it; nay would almost doubt its possibility? No where do we find a *hint*, that the least importance was attached to priest, altar, or sacrifice, except so far as they were institutions to be honored for the sake of their author. It is not surprising then, that these old Psalms continue to be the principal hymn-book of the church. Though mutilated and most imperfectly represented in the poetical versions she employs, they possess a charm, which is felt and acknowledged by every Christian heart:

Cowper, Watts, and Montgomery, may be dear to her; but still more dear, are the harpings and hallelujahs of the sweet singer of Israel!

To some, this elevated character of Old Testament piety, blended as it necessarily was in practice with so many ceremonial services, may seem difficult to explain. But we do not think so. In every age, God has made a revelation of himself to the human spirit; and when he does so, the first discovery it makes, is, that he himself is spirit, and that they who worship him must worship him in spirit, and in truth. The divinely illuminated mind needs no instruction save that which comes from the depths of its own consciousness, that the way of acceptably approaching Him, is not by thousands of rams and ten thousands of rivers of oil. Something very different is required to satisfy its felt needs, than a corporeal and local piety—the placing on an altar the fruits of the earth, and the beasts of the field; as if he who fills heaven and earth with his presence, fed on lambs, or inhaled with gratification the aroma of a slaughtered calf.

Let us prize then the heavenly treasure which has been committed to us, and with a deep feeling of privilege and responsibility, make ourselves acquainted with its contents. Love to the Old Testament Scriptures is even a test of Christian character: no man has ever drunk deep into the spirit of Jesus and his Apostles, who does not with joy draw water from these wells of salvation.

PART II.

THE INTERPRETATION OF SCRIPTURE.

HERMENEUTICS is the Science of Interpretation. Sacred hermeneutics has for its object, the holy Scriptures of the Old and New Testaments. Exegesis is the practical application of the Science. This, gives us the laws — the former executes them: thus, we speak of the *Exegesis* of a passage, according to *Hermeneutical principles.*

Before however engaging in these studies, the conscientious reader of Scripture has another work to perform—that of ascertaining the soundness of his volume. Has he a text so uncorrupted, that he may confidently rely on it as a foundation of religious belief? Has no poison been poured into the fountain? After flowing through so many countries, and being in constant contact with so much intellectual and moral impurity during the long period of three thousand years, does it send forth the same healing waters as when it first broke forth? In answering these questions, the learned assert what is called—the *Integrity* of Scripture; and a thorough examination of it in all its details and connections, is called—its *Criticism.*

The importance of this science can hardly be overrated. Whether the Horace and Plutarch that lie on our tables, faithfully represent those distinguished ancients, is a question of small practical interest; and an argument, proving beyond all doubt, that every second page was an interpolation, would hardly distress us so much as a badly-prepared breakfast. But the soundness of that awful document which contains the title-deed of our immortality, must be viewed in a very different light. No reasonable doubt should exist on such a subject, nor any pains spared to know the truth. The discussion does not however belong to our present undertaking, though it may receive slight notice before the close. That the text is in a sound state shall be assumed; and we offer our aid to the reader at the point of commencing his duties as an interpreter.

All that we purpose to say in this brief treatise, shall be arranged under two Heads:

I. We shall lay down some general Maxims, useful to be fixed in the mind as a preparation for the study;

II. Give the rules in detail by which we should be guided.

MAXIM I.

The object of Interpretation, is to give the precise thoughts which the sacred writer intended to express. No other meaning is to be sought, but that which lies in the words themselves, as he employed them: in all cases, we should take a sense *from* Scripture, rather than bring one *to* it. This rule is fundamental: and yet how often is it violated! Some, will allow no other sense but what has been baptized in their philosophy, or abstract notions of moral fitness: these, in reading the Bible, *make one* as they go. Thus, they nowhere find the doctrines of the Trinity, or Original Sin, of Atonement, Justification by Faith, or Divine Influence: some even, are unable to discover Miracles. Hence the bloody violence which they practice on everything that comes in their way. A Socinian can read the fifty-third chapter of Isaiah, without perceiving any trace of Vicarious Suffering; can turn the ἡ αρχη in the beginning of John, into the "commencement of the Christian dispensation;" and refuses to the Only Begotten of the Father, any higher diploma than that of an accomplished teacher of morals. Nothing is too absurd or arbitrary, for one who brings the word of God to the touchstone of his own speculative opinions. To such a man it is no revelation at all; for it teaches only what he knows already.

Others, make it speak invariably according to their

theological systems. When they sit down to interpret they think of nothing but what they call the "Analogy of Faith:" if the passage be explained in perfect accordance with this, all is well, and cannot be better, though Philology sweat at every pore. The Analogy of Faith is within certain limits exceedingly useful—but it has been carried entirely too far, and made to include all that a man thinks or guesses at on the subject of religion. Undoubtedly, there are certain truths in the Bible, which we are at liberty to assume, and by which we may reason analogically concerning the meaning of dubious passages. Such are the doctrines of the Unity and Perfections of God, Man's Moral Accountability, the Fall, Redemption by Grace, and Divine Influence. Any exposition of a text contradicting these, we may put down at once as disagreeing with the Analogy of Faith: the rule is a good one, and applied in the interpretation of all writers. But surely, we have no right to set up our whole system of religious belief, including the minutest of our sectarian peculiarities, as a criterion of truth! This, is to make our creed expound the word of God, instead of letting the word of God frame our creed, and establishes a principle as arbitrary and odious as that of the Socinian. Our ordinary Commentaries are greatly disfigured with the fault just mentioned—being rather dogmatical paraphrases, than expositions of Scripture itself. In few do we discover an unfettered and liberal spirit:

the Romanist, Lutheran, or Calvinist, peeping out at the end of every line.

The injury which sacred Interpretation has received from this source (artificial systems and creeds) cannot be calculated. Compared with the toils of philological investigation, they are so easy to learn, the occupation of sitting beneath the instructions of an able and eloquent polemic is so agreeable, and the preparation thus obtained for the exercises of the pulpit is so immediate and palpable, that flesh and blood can hardly resist the temptation, to elevate them above their proper level. The student giving himself to them exclusively with all the ardor of his age, is not conscious that in consequence of his abuse of them, they are leading him *right away from his Bible!* But it is often really so: its direct rays seldom reach him; the few scattered beams which strike his vision, being refracted and distorted in a greater or less degree, by the very imperfect medium through which he regards them. This is not the fault of his teacher, whose exhibition of texts may be copious and appropriate; but the effect of his own indolence, which dispenses with the labor of critical examination. The dream is certain and the interpretation sure, without betaking to his dictionary and grammar: the whole process of explaining the most obscure and difficult passage in the word of God, is to observe the place which it occupies in his *Turretine*, and Lo !—the desert smiles.

How weak such persons must be in every thing relating to the exposition of Scripture, we need not say What is still worse however, they contract a positive dislike to the business. It is foreign to all their acquired habits and modes of thinking: it demands qualifications to which they are strangers, and would compel them to sacrifice many darling conceits, which enjoy in their minds the undisputed dignity of axioms. There is no humanly constructed creed of any length, which does not exhibit partial and contracted views. The truths of Scripture are not capable of exact scientific definition: they are the ideas of the Divine Mind; and like that Mind possess a certain *boundlessness*, which disdains to be cramped by artificial moulds—resembling the sublime and beautiful in nature, which awaken sentiment and interest the affections, but are of too delicate a texture, to be compressed into scholastic arrangements. Accordingly, we find the sacred writers never attempting to give a precise dialectic form to their statements. The noble and affecting thoughts with which they are penetrated undergo no pruning process, nor are they subjected to metaphysical analysis: they are not drawn out into regular propositions, but are poured forth with the same divine negligence, with which they presented themselves to their spiritually enlightened minds. Nothing indeed is more remarkable than the artlessness—the charming and yet sublime simplicity, which characterize these holy men. When they have a truth to announce, there is no indication of holding back in order to give it with philosophical exactness—no betrayal of a fear, that unless infinite care be taken, it will not dovetail with some other truth that has been announced previously, giving a writer the appearance of a man treading among pit-falls and spring-guns. They walk with a bold freedom, of which every movement proves their consciousness; shoving aside in their onward march, the whole troop of collaterals, trampling on contradictions, and anxious only to express themselves on the subject immediately before them, with appropriate energy. The man who undertakes to interpret them, must catch their spirit in this respect, or they will receive small justice at his hands.

MAXIM II.

The same method must be followed in expounding Scripture, which we employ in searching out the meaning of other books. It was indited to men; it speaks to men, in the language of men; and was understood by those to whom in ancient times it was addressed, as they understood any other communication. The design of God in giving it, was to communicate certain ideas—in order to which, he must speak to us, *just as do others.* Words call up ideas, not by any native significance, but by compact, and every one in speaking is supposed to conform to the bargain. If he does not, but employs language in a sense different from that established by common use, he is, to all intents and purposes, a Covenant Breaker. In reading Scripture, therefore, we are to use the same appliances and aids employed in other cases. Inspiration gives it no special privileges: rather may we suppose, that a revelation of God's will to the great world of mankind, must be peculiarly susceptible of popular interpretation, and positively require it. This rule sweeps away at once a host of errors: we shall specify two.

1st. That of the Papists, who contend that the Exposition of Scripture is entirely *sui generis*, and supernatural—being committed to Holy Mother Church, consisting of the Pope, Decrees of Councils, and the ancient Fathers. The pretension is rejected by all sound Protestants with disgust. While we say that the Bible is the book of God, we affirm with equal emphasis, that it is the *Book of Man*, and can be understood by man in the use of the ordinary means. We also affirm that Holy Mother, with her Councils and Fathers, has given too many proofs of something worse than mere fallibility, to be entrusted with the authoritative exposition of it. The Patristic interpretations of Scripture are, with a few exceptions, contemptible. Jerome, Theodoret, and Chrysostom, are all that a modern can quote, and absurdities of every kind are found even in them: they were all ignorant of Hebrew, except Jerome, and the later Fathers knew little of Greek. When they used citations in controversy, they took anything (as Jerome himself acknowledges) which seemed likely to confound their opponents; and there was scarcely one, who did not prefer an allegorical explanation, or some frigid and far-fetched conceit, to the plain sense of a passage.

2dly. The errors of Fanatics and Enthusiasts; such as Quakers and Swedenborgians, who boast of certain immediate revelations, which they call the "*Word of God within.*" This interior light is the supreme rule, which entirely dispenses with every thing else—with the knowledge of languages, philosophy, logic, and common sense. With it, every shoe-black is abundantly qualified to expound all mysteries: without it, "all the learning in the world," says the famous Barclay, "will only make light darkness, and turn the truth into a lie." How the Bible fares in such hands, their writings show. Yet it would be folly to reason with such people. They are above reason: theirs, is the little Goshen where all true light is found: darkness blacker than that of Egypt covers the whole world without.

MAXIM III.

The sense of Scripture is (in general) ONE: *in other words, we are not to assign many meanings to a passage.* Words indeed, have a variety of significations; but they cannot have this variety at the same time. A single sense must be chosen, in doing which, one expositor may differ from another, and it may be dubious which is right. They cannot, however, be *both right:* if we approve the one, we must, if they really differ, disapprove the other.

The transgressors of this rule, are the Mystics and Allegorists. Their fundamental maxim is not unlike that of the Papists; for they consider the Bible to be a book so different from others, that its depth of meaning can never be reached by the ordinary laws of interpretation. Being from God, they insist that it must in all respects be worthy of him, and contain a richness of thought suited to his infinite understanding. Hence their favorite maxim; *Verba Scripturæ tantum ubique significare, quantum significare possunt:* i. e. whatever a word *may* mean, it *does* mean. A single noun could thus have twenty different senses in the same place, and refer to twenty different things. This odd theory was a great favorite with the Jews in the time of our Lord and his apostles, who occasionally allegorized to please them, though by no means frequently. See an instance in Gal. iv. 22; where the Apostle makes Sarah and Hagar types of the two covenants. So far did the Jews carry their love of it, that their rabbis all maintained—"There is not a letter in Scripture, or apex of a letter, which does not contain whole mountains of meaning." They even had a science or art, called the Caballa which by changing, disjoining, or transposing letters, or by calculating their value as arithmetical signs, elicited worlds of profound mystery.

The Jews communicated their mania to the old Christian Fathers, whose writings abound in mystical expositions of all kinds. Everything in sacred history, was metamorphosed into type and symbol. Origen denied even the literal truth of history, contending that its whole and only meaning was allegorical. Thus he pronounced it absolutely absurd to suppose, that the world was created in six days: the creation signified the renovation of the soul by the Gospel, and the six days intimate that it is carried on by degrees. Israel in Egypt, he makes to be the soul living in error; and the seven plagues are its purgations from various evil habits—the frogs denoting loquacity, the flies carnal appetites, the boils pride and arrogance, &c. This mode of expounding continued through the different ages of the church, and has been formally adopted by the Papists, who recognize three different senses besides the literal, viz. the allegorical, tropological, and analogical. Nor was it put down by the reformation. Cocceius, a celebrated Dutch divine, carried it almost as far as Origen did. He held that the whole of the Old Testament was an anticipative history of the Christian church, containing a full recital of every thing which should happen to the end of time. Even the Lord's Prayer is a prophesy, and its six parts denote six great epochs in history. Every good man in the Old Testament, is a type of Christ, or his apostles: Every bad man, of the devil, or the unbelieving Jews.

Such schemes are to be utterly rejected. They destroy all certainty of interpretation: taking the ground from beneath our feet; and making Scripture a nose of wax which every one may twist into the shape that pleases him best. Thomas Woolston, a celebrated English infidel, attacked Christianity itself with these arms, insisting that the narratives of Christ's miracles were not designed to be histories, but are pure allegories. Volney, a French writer, has turned the evangelic history into a system of astronomy—Christ being the sun and moon, and the twelve apostles the twelve signs of the zodiac. Without affirming that there are no secondary senses in Scripture we believe that (the phrase being properly understood) there are very few. Generally, the meaning is, as in other books, *one;* and that lies near the surface. Who ever heard of a man in common conversation, attaching different significations to the words he used—unless indeed he was playing a game at riddles, or *double* entendres?

MAXIM IV.

The interpretation of Scripture requires suitable preparation. The languages in which it is written, are strange—difficult; and both are dead. In every page, there are references to times, places, transactions, with which we must be well acquainted. The history of the world is given, with a few breaks and interruptions, from the beginning to the four thousandth year. Not only are there accounts of the Hebrew nation, but of many others with whom war or peaceful intercourse brought them in connection; Syrians, Egyptians, Assyrians, Persians, Greeks, Romans: cities, lakes, rivers, hills, valleys, are continually mentioned. So are natural productions—as plants, trees, precious stones, animals. Hence arises the necessity of being well acquainted with—

1st. Hebrew and Greek: and also the cognate languages, Chaldee and Latin.

2d. History, civil and political; especially of the Israelites, Egyptians, Phœnicians, Assyrians, and Greeks. If the student has no time for extensive investigation, he should at least make himself master of Josephus and Prideaux, who are accessible to all, and full of entertainment as well as instruction.

3d. Chronology; which ascertains the dates and order of events. There is great uncertainty and difficulty in this science, but it must not be neglected. A general knowledge of its principles, and a clear view of the great epochs into which sacred and profane history is divided, with an ability to refer every important transaction to its proper time, is indispensable. Chronology is one of the eyes of history; the other is—

4th. Geography. That of Palestine is of special moment, for obvious reasons: but that of Egypt, Idumea, Arabia, and Mesopotamia, must not be passed by.

5th. Customs and manners, or archaiology. These exercise a mighty influence on the ideas of a people, and their mode of expressing them. There is in Scripture, a constant allusion to Hebrew usages, and nearly all its tropes are borrowed from them, in connection with the natural features of the country.

The importance of a sound acquaintance with this branch of knowledge, and also the last, (geography), cannot be too deeply impressed on the mind of the student. No man is fit to expound a paragraph in any book whatever, unless he can bring distinctly before his mind all the usages and historical facts, all the circumstances of time and place, which relate to the subject treated. This is necessary even to understand it, but much more to receive those strong impressions which excite the sensibility. Every one who has attended to the laws of thought, knows how wonderfully our conceptions are enlivened by association with local scenes and circumstances. A man of general reading may, at his fire-side, call up pleasant reminiscences of Greece, and the various glorious events recorded in her history: but how tame his thoughts, compared with those which possess the accomplished scholar who has trod her soil, and seen all that remains to her, or by the constant perusal of her writers, has made himself as familiar with every hill and valley, as if he had seen them with his bodily eyes. It is a common remark of historians concerning the Christians of the middle ages, that their devotion was astonishingly increased by a pilgrimage to Holy Land. The must lukewarm usually returned full of faith and fervor. This might be expected. They had gone over the hallowed ground, and were able to form a distinct picture of it. They had walked the streets of the city which their Divine Saviour had honored with his ministrations, and trod the very mount on which he had been lifted up between heaven and earth. The vivid idea of the localities, passed by an easy transition to all the facts and doctrines connected with them, and the felt reality of Calvary, diffused itself over the sufferings which a thousand years before had been endured there. In a word, the sensible ideas of time and place became so incorporated with their religious belief, as to form one complex whole—and they thought as little of questioning the truth of their creed as the reality of their perceptions.

It is true, that few of us may be able to test the principle just stated by visiting the sacred land in person. Much, however, can be effected by a thorough course of reading. Let the student take into his hand "Jahn's Archæology," with an Ancient Geography and Atlas, studying at the same time Robinson's "Biblical Researches," he will be surprised to find what a vivifying and warming influence they will exert, not only over his imagination, but his heart. The simplest narrative of Scripture will be read with an enthusiastic interest, of which he had previously no conceptions; and even its doctrines be clothed with a new attractiveness.

6th. Logic and general literature; which invigorate the mind, and inure to habits of accurate discrimination. Every study that improves the thinking faculties —especially the judgment, and enlarges our mental horizon, will make its value felt in explaining the word of God. What blunders have been committed by commentators, simply because they did not know that they were reading poetry; and who would not have been benefitted by the discovery, as they knew nothing of the laws of that kind of composition—their whole reading having been confined to the mellifluous jingle of Dr. Watts! The remark of Cicero concerning the orator, is quite as true of the sacred interpreter: "Quod debet omnibus disciplinis instructus esse." Let no student of theology allow himself to think, that when he occasionally, or even frequently, opens the page of a Milton or a Locke, he is wasting time, or stealing it away from his proper work.

7th. Above all, sincere and ardent piety. Without this, no learning and acuteness will secure the interpreter from shamefully blundering on the very threshhold of his undertaking, nor from a constant succession of blunders to the end. His heart must be attuned to his sacred employment—by a profound conviction of ignorance and guilt, by sincere love to God, and a devout longing toward every thing that is holy and divine; by willingness to put himself absolutely and without reserve at the feet of his great teacher; in short, by such a sympathy between his spirit and the spirit of Christ, that he can enter into the very thoughts of Christ, and expound them by a sort of divine intuition. There is a deep philosophy, (ignorance of which is the rock on which many interpreters have made shipwreck), in the promise: "I will put my laws in their mind, and write them in their hearts, and they shall not teach every man his neighbor, saying, know the Lord; for all shall know me from the least to the greatest." The meaning is not, that under the new and spiritual dispensation of the Gospel to which the promise refers, external methods of instruction will be done away; but that it will be no more a *hard, up-hill* work—as it always is, when the hearts of men are not in harmony with their employment. In consequence of the holy congeniality of the inner man with the objective revelation, the latter will be received with such ardent, whole-souled affection at the very moment of being presented, that the outward teaching will be scarcely remembered.

Illustrations of this are found all around: let one example serve. How slow to learn, is the boy whose tastes and inclinations have no sympathy with the object of his study! Like the ass, he needs a constant whip, to maintain a faint appearance of locomotion: even the tender, all-hoping mother has ceased to plead for him, and concurs in the universal judgment that he is an incorrigible dunce. But take him from his ungrateful toil, and task his energies with a work which interests his affections, the almost idiot expands into a young intellectual giant, and his proficiency astonishes all observers. So it is with the true Christian. Before he experienced the power of religion, nothing was more difficult than his indoctrination in those great truths that form the life and soul of evangelical piety. He complained that they were entirely wanting in evidence, as well as devoid of attraction. He could not apprehend their meaning: his memory failed in the endeavor to retain them, and a sermon in which any of them was discussed, invariably put him to sleep: no distillation of henbane or poppy equalled it in narcotic virtue, But how prodigious the change! All is now light, clearness and beauty. The doctrines which occasioned him so much perplexity are now as easy and simple to his understanding, as they are refreshing to his heart. He scarcely needs a hermeneutical apparatus, but at once drinks them in with all the zest and facility, with which the infant—*heaven-taught*—draws its natural aliment from the mother's breast. This is what the pious Psalmist alludes to when he says, "I have more understanding than all my teachers: he had just before given the explanation,—"Oh how *I love thy law.*"

We proceed to the Special Rules which should guide us in the interpretation of Scripture.

RULE I.

Carefully investigate the Usus loquendi. By this is meant what the words literally express, the *custom of speech.* The meaning of words is for the most part perfectly arbitrary. They call up certain ideas, because men have agreed that they shall do so, and for no other reason: general usage, therefore, is the great standard, "quem penes arbitrium est et jus et norma dicendi." In living languages, we ascertain the usage from conversation and personal intercourse. In those long since dead, as the Hebrew and Greek, we draw on various sources:

1st. Contemporary writers. With respect to the Old Testament, we have none such—all the Hebrew extant being contained in our volume. In place of them we have a tolerably clear and ample Jewish tradition: for it cannot be doubted, that the rabbis have preserved with good fidelity much of their old national language. As to the New Testament, we have all the Greek writers from Homer to Longinus; though they must be used with caution, as the New Testament is written in a Hebraistic idiom, and not in the classical language of Demosthenes.

2d. Scholiasts and glossographers. These were men who lived after the death of the writers; but while the language was still living, and who must have understood the meaning of words better than we. Scholia, were short notes inserted in the margin of the work explained, illustrating some phrase or turn of expression. Scholia on the New Testament are very numerous, and some of them have come down from remote antiquity. A noble edition of the New Testament, containing a large collection of them, has been published by Matthai, a distinguished German professor. Glossaries (from γλωσσα a form of speech) are dictionaries, giving explanations of certain words arranged in alphabetical order, and differing from common dictionaries in this, that they contain remarks on such words only as are difficult, and obscure. The principal works of this kind are those of Hesychius, Suidas, Phavorinus, and Photius.

3d. Ancient translations, made when the languages were still living. Such is the Septuagint version of the Hebrew Bible, made nearly three hundred years before Christ; when the language was well understood, though not spoken with perfect purity. The value of this work to the student of the New Testament, as well as the Old, is incalculable: for without the steady light which is cast by it on the meaning and force of expressions, the interpreter could scarcely advance a step. The Chaldee paraphrase, is another venerable translation of the Old Testament. It presents the views concerning the meaning of that part of Scripture, entertained by the learned Jews contemporary with our Lord: being composed a little before his birth, and in the dialect spoken at that time by the nation. The old Syriac version is also extremely valuable.

4th. Kindred dialects. This source of aid is peculiarly useful with respect to that part of Scripture which most needs it—the Old Testament. The Hebrew has three sisters, so like her, that there can be no mistake as to their common parentage: they are the Arabic, Chaldaic or East Armaean, Syriac or West Armaean. In two of these—the Syriac and Arabic—there are numerous writings still extant, and the Arabic is a living language. The use of dialects in determining the sense of words, requires skill and judgment; as it by no means follows that the precise signification is the same in both, because they are sisters. Yet its great value as a subsidiary, is generally confessed: proofs of it you have in every page of Gesenius's dictionary.

5th. Etymology; or the examination of roots.—When other expedients fail, we may sometimes derive considerable assistance from tracing an expression to its original element. But after all, etymology is slippery ground. Words in the process of derivation or composition, often deviate from their original import, so that the child loses nearly all resemblance to its parent. Thus the English word *villain*, in our old writers means a *slave; rascal*, in Saxon, a *lean beast; hostis*, in Latin, originally signified, (according to Cicero,) a *stranger; pagan*, which with us is equivalent to *heathen*, and denoted nothing worse in the language last mentioned from which we obtained it, than a *farmer*, or inhabitant of the country. קָדֵשׁ is a Hebrew verb signifying *to be holy;* the noun קָדֵשָׁה, one of its derivatives, is the common term for *prostitute*. Two instances may be given from the New Testament, to illustrate the danger of reasoning from etymological significations. The verb προγινωσκω, is compounded of the preposition προ, *before*, and γινοκω, *to know*. It should therefore always denote simple foreknowledge, and many Arminians contend that it does so; yet whoever impartially examines the usus loquendi of the New Testament, will see at once, that it is sometimes fully equal in strength of meaning to our English word *foreordain*: see Rom. ii. 2, Acts ii. 23, 1 Pet. i. 20. The adjective αιωνιο, is commonly used by the Greeks for "eternal" or "everlasting," and is the strongest term they can employ: in this sense it is constantly used in the New Testament, with perhaps one or two exceptions. But the Universalist reminds us that it comes from αιων *an age*, and must therefore be translated "*having age*," or "*enduring for an age.*" So too, αιωνες αιωνων can mean nothing more than a "number of ages," though in every case, without a solitary exception, it expresses proper eternity.

We cannot forbear citing another example of deserting the established meaning of words or phrases for supposed etymologies, from a Scottish Divine of some note, who has written on the Baptist controversy. The Rev. Mr. Ewing author of a Greek Dictionary and Grammar, dissatisfied with the usual method of meeting the Immersionists, undertakes to show that the word *baptize*—so far from signifying to "dip" or "merge," properly denotes the operation of "dropping" or "sprinkling;" and accomplishes it in the following way. All Greek verbs, being derived from biliteral roots (he had probably heard of this theory without understanding it) the word βαπτω of which βαπτιζω is a form, must be traced to the syllable *bap* or *pap*, which is of course equivalent to the English *pop*. But *pop* is a word evidently taken from nature, and expresses the sound of a drop of water falling upon a table. βαπτω therefore means the same thing, and represents very happily the sprinkling process; so that when the Apostles were commanded to "go and disciple all nations, baptizing them in the name," &c. they were required in so many words to admit converts into the visible church by *bopping* or *popping* on them—*quod erat demonstrandum!* We would not take notice of a hypothesis so unutterably ludicrous, were it not calculated by its very ludicrousness to fix in the mind an important principle of interpretation. We are far from sympathizing with our Baptist friends in their strong dislike to aspersion. On the contrary, we think that in their zeal for carrying out the physical idea of *mersion*, they forget that by a not uncommon extension of meaning, the physical act when employed as a *mere symbol*, may lose much of its water, and express religious ablution in general; of which fair examples may be quoted from the New Testament. At the same time, we grant that some of the arguments employed by our writers are extremely puerile, and would try the temper of persons much more disposed to play the amiable than our worthy brethren seem to be, where their distinctive practice is concerned.

Nothing can be more unsafe than the modes of procedure referred to in the three preceding examples. Independently of the fact, that what we assign as the original signification may be false (which the last instance strikingly illustrates) the use of words is continually fluctuating, and we cannot be too careful in guarding against errors from this source. Yet they are common: whole systems of theology, and even natural science, have been constructed on fanciful etymologies, by men whose imaginations outran their judgment, of which we may cite Parkhurst's Hebrew and Greek lexicons as an example. Great aid, however, may be derived from a sober and skilful tracing of words back to their source: if it does not always direct to their present meaning, it seldom fails to throw a happy light on the history of language.

These are the principal means of the "Usus Loquendi." It would be cruel, however, to impose upon all, the task of digging into these deep mines. The labor is in a measure saved by good dictionaries, which, if really good, contain the results of such investigations. Happily we are well supplied with Gesenius in Hebrew, and Wahl and Bretschneider in Greek: Professor Robinson's Lexicon is also excellent, combining the good qualities of both.

RULE II.

Examine carefully the parallel passages. By these are meant, texts which relate to the same subject, teach the same doctrine, or relate the same historical fact. They should be accurately collated, that one may supply light to the other, and fill up what is wanting to the perspicuity of the whole. We perform this operation constantly—in reading the most familiar letter, or the simplest story. Its value in the study and explanation of scripture, can hardly be expressed. It not only enables us to enter into the meaning and force of particular expressions, but places us on a commanding eminence, where we may survey the whole field of divine truth, and admire the harmony of its several parts. All systematic theology should be built on this alone. "I will not scruple to assert," says the learned Bishop Horsley, "that the most illiterate Christian, if he can but read his English Bible, and will take the pains to read it in this manner, (studying the parallel passages) without any other commentary than what the different parts mutually furnish for each other, will not only attain all that practical knowledge which is necessary to salvation, but will become learned in every thing relating to his religion. He may safely be ignorant of all philosophy, and all history, which he does not find in the sacred books."

Parallels are of two kinds, *Verbal*, and *Real; Verbal*, are those in which the very same word or phrase is used, though the meaning in one may be much clearer than in the other, and consequently give light to it. Thus in Joel ii. 28, God promises that he "will pour out his Spirit on all flesh." Doubtful how to understand "flesh" in this passage, I compare it with Gen. vi. 12, which says that "all flesh corrupted their way." As the whole mass of mankind is here meant, I feel authorized to give the same extent of meaning to the word in Joel. In Matt. i. 20, the angel of the Lord declares that Mary shall "conceive of the Holy Ghost." Struck with the peculiarity of the expression, I go to the corresponding passage in Luke, and find him using it also, but, adding another which is evidently intended to be exegetical, viz, "Power of the Highest," Luke i. 35: The Holy Ghost therefore is here equivalent to the Divine energy. In 1 Cor. vii. 1, Paul says "It is not good for a man to marry." A little startled at this squinting of the great apostle towards monkery, I look further down the chapter for an explanation, and find it in the 26th verse; "it is good for the present distress." Marriage is an excellent thing, but may be very inexpedient in times of severe persecution.

Real parallelism is a correspondence in the thought or subject, although the words are different; and is still more important than the other. It is two-fold, *historical* and *doctrinal*. *Historical* parallelisms are those which occur in the relation of matters of fact. The four Gospels are full of these, and a careful collation of them is of unspeakable use in interpretation. One evangelist fills up the outlines briefly sketched by another, supplying some circumstance of time, place, or occasion, which throw a flood of light on the whole transaction. From a diligent and minute comparison of their accounts, Harmonies are constructed, which deserve to be well studied. There are similar coincidences in the Old Testament, ex. gr. between the books of Chronicles and Kings.

Many of these passages offer serious difficulty to the interpreter, in consequence of a strong appearance of inconsistency and contradiction. The greater number however, yield readily to diligent and careful scrutiny—originating in some misconception of the reader, or in false readings of the text; which in the Old Testament are numerous. By taking a correct view of the subject, scope, and connection of each passage, and observing the style, with other peculiarities of the writers, discrepancies which at first appeared with a most fierce and threatening aspect, have turned into lambs and doves. Some however, (especially those found in the Gospel narratives), are really perplexing, and have been the "crux theologorum" in all ages: of which we cite the following as illustrations. There seems a very decided repugnance between Matthew's account of our Saviour's baptism, and that of John; the former representing the Baptist as knowing Jesus from the first, while the latter says that he did not know him till the descent of the Spirit. Compare John i. 33 and Matthew iii. 13. There is also a singular clashing between the narratives of Matthew and Luke concerning the miracle wrought upon the blind near Jericho—Matthew making the number, *two;* and expressly saying that our Lord was departing "*from* the city"—Luke declaring that he was going *to* it, and that but *one* individual was restored: Compare Matthew xx. 30 and Luke xviii. 35. In his account of the crucifixion, John differs from the other evangelists as to time, stating, that it took place after the *sixth* hour; Mark with whom Matthew and Luke agree, names the *third.* In the accounts of his unction by Mary, the discordancy is equally marked—John saying that it occurred *six* days before the Passover;

Matthew and Mark specifying *two*. The narratives of Christ's resurrection and the circumstances which followed it seem also at variance, and in no small degree.

These examples will suffice, though we might adduce a score of others. Now it is not allowed for a moment that they are incapable of being harmonized: still, it cannot be denied that they bear a strong appearance of discrepancy. The student therefore should examine them carefully, with such helps as the learned have furnished; remembering that he must occasionally fall in with the infidel—and that the infidel is an insect of the blue bottle genus who always settles on such spots. If after his best exertions he does not receive perfect satisfaction, let him not be frightened, as if these gentlemen had gained a fearful advantage: the truth is, they have gained a loss—the fact of disagreement in matters of trifling moment proving triumphantly the substantial veracity of our writers, and the consequent truth of Christianity. Whatever trouble it may give us in defending the doctrine of verbal inspiration, it is a thunderbolt against the Deist: for is it not certain, that if the sacred historians had combined to palm a falsehood on us, they would like fraudulent gamesters have taken care to play into each other's hands, and studiously avoided every appearance of collision? But nothing of this kind appears. There is no leaning on each other—no mutual adjustment of what they have to say, nor endeavor so to trim their statements that they shall nicely fit those of their colleagues, and the whole together present, like fine cabinet work, a smooth unbroken surface to the eye. What a delightful proof of the unbending and uncompromising honesty of these pure-hearted men! Remember these things, Christian student; and when any of the difficulties alluded to rise up to harass and perplex you, take comfort from reflecting—that the occassion of your distress is one of the strongest guarantees for the truth of your religion. Bless God that there are things in the Gospel *which you are called to reconcile!*

Parallelism of *doctrine* is found, where the same principles are taught in two or more passages. The great business of the didactic theologian is to investigate this class of correspondencies. All sound knowledge of Christian doctrines, depends on the faithful and judicious comparison of scripture with scripture. Does the student want clear views concerning man's relations to his Creator, original corruption, the person and work of the Redeemer, justification, the connection between it and the renewal of the soul in holiness, the happiness and misery of a future state—his course is plain and easy. He must find the great classical passages on each point, and bring them in juxtaposition: he must compare (asking no other assistance but God's grace and a good dictionary,) Isaiah with Matthew, Paul to the Romans with Paul to the Galatians, and both these with James—the author of the Apocalypse with Daniel and Ezekiel, the Epistle to the Hebrews with Genesis and Leviticus. Let him do this in fear of the Lord, with a single desire to know the truth ;.he will not probably come from his labor a hair splitting metaphysician or cunning rhetorician—but he will prove something more and better, "a good steward of the manifold grace of God."

Besides the coincidences above-mentioned, there is in scripture what is called the *poetic parallelism*, with which every reader of Hebrew is acquainted. It consists in a mutual correspondence of the two members of a stanza; the one being a sort of echo to the other, as in Isaiah i. 3:

The ox knoweth his owner,
The ass his master's crib,
Israel does not know,
My people do not consider.

Sometimes the answering clause is synonymous with the first, as in the example just cited.

Sometimes antithetical, or opposed to it, as in Prov. xii. 1:

A wise son makes a glad father,
But a foolish son is the grief of his mother.

At others, it contains only a farther development of the thought, as in Psal. cxlviii. 7:

Praise the Lord upon the earth,
Ye dragons and all deeps;
Fire and hail: snow and vapour;
Stormy wind; fulfilling his will:
Mountains and all hills:
Fruit trees and all cedars.

These parallelisms are of excellent use to the interpreter. They often enable him to decide important questicns concerning the meaning of•words and propositions, when deserted by all other hermeneutical aids. Nor is their use confined to the Old Testament. The same rythmical construction everywhere prevails in the New, which in this, as in many other respects, has received a decided tinge from the Hebrew writings. On this whole subject we earnestly recommend to the student, Bishop Lowth's Lectures on Hebrew Poetry, a book almost worthy of its theme.

RULE III.

The consideration of the author's scope or design greatly facilitates interpretation. Every man (not a fool,) has some definite purpose in speaking, and it is fairly presumed that he will use such terms and arguments as are suited to it. The scope is the soul—the vis vitæ of a work, which lives and breathes through the whole, giving order, force and beauty to every part It may be ascertained in various ways.

1. *By marking the occasion on which the passage or book was written.* Thus the occasion of Paul's epistle to the Galatians, was the dissemination among them of Jewish errors concerning the way of justification: he "marvels that they were so soon removed

from him that called them into the grace of the Gospel." The epistles to the Romans had a like origin. The inscriptions on many of the Psalms, describing the condition of the poet when they were composed, give them wonderful vivacity and impressiveness: we almost seem to be reading different compositions. Take for example the third Psalm, and in reading it, set before you the pious monarch driven from his throne by the machinations of an unnatural son, and wandering among the hills of Gilead, wanting the very necessaries of life, and in constant danger from enemies who were thirsting for his blood; yet expressing his perfect confidence that all would be well at last, whatever temporary triumph might be allowed them. How thrilling every expression of his victorious faith in the power and promise of God under such circumstances! It appears that the serene old man did not lose a night's rest in the darkest period of his trial:

> I lay me down and sleep
> I awake for Jehovah sustains me,
> I fear not ten thousands of people,
> Who set themselves round about me.

The discourses of Christ receive like illustrations, from adverting to the occasion of them. Many were answers to the cavils and impertinencies of the Pharisees: some were connected with occurrences which took place in his presence: others were suggested by questions of his disciples. How much we should lose of the meaning and beauty of his conversation with the Samaritan woman, if we separated it from the little introductory circumstances which are recorded; viz. that the place was "Sychar," the chief city of the most bitter enemies of his nation; that "Jacob's well" was there; that weary with journeying he sat upon its mouth waiting the return of his disciples, "who had gone into the city to buy meat;" that he excited her astonishment by asking drink of her, "for the Jews have no dealings with the Samaritans." Every one of these apparently trifling incidents has its use in illustrating what follows: not one could be spared, without detracting from a composition which measured by a standard merely literary, has nothing to compare with it in all the ancient and modern classics.

2. *By examining whether the writer has not himself mentioned his design.* Thus the Evangelist John informs us, what his purpose was in writing his gospel, John xx. 31. "These things are written that ye might believe upon Jesus, and that believing ye might have life through his name." Luke avows his design very clearly. He seems to have been dissatisfied with some of the current accounts which had been published of the life of Christ, and determines to give an accurate and orderly detail, the result of his own personal investigations. As he intimates his purpose to write καθεξης, i. e. "in order"—having care fully followed up every event, παρηκολουθηκοτι ανωθεν

ακριβως many judicious commentators infer that where the evangelists differ as to the order of facts, his account is to be preferred, and have accordingly made it the basis of their schemes of harmony. The author of Ecclesiastes is another instance of a sacred writer who states his object. The whole work is a commentary on the first verse, "Vanity of vanities," saith the preacher; all is vanity." It must be confessed that he sticks to his melancholy text most closely, and expounds it with a fearful energy.

Occasionally, a sacred writer gives his purpose not at the outset, but the close of his remarks. A striking instance is found in Paul's epistle to the Romans. In the first three chapters, he elaborately reviews the moral condition of mankind both Jews and Gentiles, in all ages, and shows that the whole world was guilty before God. In the 20th verse of the third chapter, we see him distinctly approaching his object: "Therefore by the deeds of the law shall no flesh be justified in his sight; for by the law is the knowledge of sin." This was one point gained, and one of momentous interest to a mind anxiously inquiring, "How shall man be just with God." But he had a much higher aim than merely to prostrate the sinner: he kills that he may make alive; and after an eloquent discussion through the seven verses that follow, brings out in the 28th, the great central truth of the Gospel with dialectic formality. "Therefore we conclude that a man is justified by faith without the deeds of the law."

3dly. If both the expedients mentioned fail, we *should read the whole book, marking the coherence of its various parts.* Mr. Locke recommends the perusal of it at one sitting, quoting his own experience in favor of the plan. "I concluded it necessary," he says, (speaking of Paul's epistles), "for the understanding of any one of them, often to read it all through at one sitting, and to observe as well as I could, the design of his writing it. If the first reading gave me some light, the second gave me more; and so I persisted on, reading constantly the whole epistle over at once, till I came to have a good general view of the apostle's main purpose in writing." The advice is excellent, suggesting the very method we employ in ascertaining the scope of other writings. If the title-page leave any doubt or darkness on the subject, we instinctively turn to the table of contents, or skim over the different chapters, before we engage in a critical perusal. We thus catch the author's drift—we see what *he would be at*—without some knowledge of which, reading is the most intolerable of all drudgery.

RULE IV.

Examine well what precedes and follows the part to be expounded. This is called the *context;* and is divided into the *remote* and *immediate*. The *immediate*, is that part which stands in immediate proximity to the passage; the *remote*, may extend some distance backward and forward. The mind generally thinks in train, and connects its ideas together by well-known laws of association. This connection of thought, and the logical relation of one part of the series to another, is an invaluable key to the mind of a writer, except when he professedly deals in aphorisms; as the author of the book of Proverbs, and Christ in part of his sermon on the mount. It is in some respects more important than the scope: the latter only gives me the author's general purpose, which does not forbid the admission of episodes, and topics merely collateral: We shall be certain to err with regard to these, if we neglect the connection.

We must be on our guard, however, against *manufacturing* a connection; in other words against putting a false construction on what precedes or follows, and then moulding the exposition in conformity with our own gloss,—a fault often committed. Falsehood can only beget falsehood. Nor, supposing that our construction is true, may we adjust our passage to it by any violation of the Usus Loquendi, or rules of grammar. In these cases, we must take what might seem the worst of two meanings—sacrificing contextual symmetry to the general laws of language. Thus limited, the rule that no explanation is to be admitted which does not suit the context, is of constant use.

Suppose me reading the 42d Psalm, and considering the pathetic exclamation in the second verse:

> My soul thirsteth for God, the living God,
> When shall I come and appear before God;
> My tears are my meat day and night,
> While it is said continually, Where is thy God?

My first impulse is to view it as the expression of a wish to die and enjoy the felicity of heaven; especially as the phrase "seeing God," often refers to future blessedness. But a glance at the 4th verse, shows that the pious monarch longed for restoration to the services of the earthly sanctuary, of which he had been deprived by the persecutions of his son Absalom:

> When I think of this, I pour out my heart in tears,
> How I went with the multitude—went to the house of God,
> With jubilee and praise in a sacred happy throng.

The 110th Psalm describes the victorious progress of an illustrious prince, greatly honored by God, and exalted to his right hand. The first three verses leave me in doubt whether the poet speaks of David or another and far greater personage, as the sitting at God's right hand may be figurative:

> Jehovah said unto my Lord,
> Sit thou at my right hand,
> Until I make thine enemies thy footstool,

> Thy powerful sceptre Jehovah sends out of Zion.
> Rule in the midst of thy foes.

But the 4th verse settles the question :

> Jehovah hath sworn and will not repent,
> Thou art an everlasting priest,
> Of the order of Melchisedec.

David was no priest, nor could any Hebrew monarch assume the office without heaven-daring profanity. The strange and (to the Jew) astounding phenomenon of a "priest upon a throne," directs us at once to David's Son and *Lord*. The application of this simple test will enable the plainest Christian to detect the Psalms called Messianic, at a glance. They all embody in their representations such remarkable incidents and traits of personal character, as make it impossible to apply them without the grossest impropriety to any but the anointed of the Father. Let the 2d, 16th, 22d, 45th, and 72d be brought to this touchstone; nothing but arrant infidelity can resist the force of the argument.

It may admit a doubt whether the celebrated description in Rom. vii. of the struggle between the "flesh and the spirit," refers to the true Christian or the unregenerate. There are some expressions in it, which certaitnty agree best with the latter supposition. On the other hand, there are whole sentences which cannot at all be reconciled with this hypothesis, and compel us to understand the apostle as describing the exercises of the Christian. In the 18th verse, it is clearly implied that the person described, possesses impulses and principles superior to those of unrenewed nature. "In me, that is, in my flesh, dwelleth no good thing." In the 22d verse, he is said to "delight in the Law of God after the inner man;" and in the 25th, he thanks God for "his deliverance through Christ Jesus." Farther, to entirely preclude the supposition that this deliverance is a *new state*, following, and not contemporary with the struggle, he adds, "So then with the *mind* I serve the Law of God; but with the *flesh* the law of sin." Surely it is not in accordance with the tenor of scripture, as an excellent commentator observes, to describe in this way the exercises and character of unholy men.

Let us bring to the contextual touchstone another passage—the well-known paragraph in Romans 5th, which seems to assert a direct causal connection, between Adam and his posterity. "By one man sin entered into the world, and death by sin, and so death passed upon all men, for all have sinned:" "By one man's offence, death reigned by one:" "By the offence of one, judgment came upon all to condemnation:" "By one man's disobedience, many were made sinners." Pelagians affirm, that all intended by these remarkable statements is, that Adam gave the first example of sinning, and that *somehow*, his posterity walked in his steps. They compare the phraseology with expressions like these: "By Sir Robert Walpole, bribery and corruption entered the British parliament:" "By Lysander, luxury entered Sparta;" which, according to them, only mean that the evils mentioned began with these persons. Without dwelling on the violence done to the words by this gloss, or the fact that their own phrases clearly denote not only a chronological but a *causal* connection, let the student look at the whole series of discourse that follows; in which the apostle, with an emphasis and accumulation of synonymous expressions, which show how intently his mind was working with the thought, draws a parallel between Adam and the Redeemer. If he does not mean to say that there was a similitude between them in official character and relations, almost perfect, there is no meaning in language. The inference is irresistible. Christ was not the first who received salvation, but is the immediate *author* of it. In the same sense our guilty progenitor is the immediate author of sin and misery to our world.

This attempt to explain away the plain meaning of scripture is sufficiently gross. That of the Socinians to evacuate the Epistle to the Hebrews of our Redeemer's Priesthood and atonement, is yet more so. The priesthood of Jesus, they say, is a bold figure, merely denoting that he was a consecrated minister of God. His sacrifice consisted in the virtuous obedience which he yielded, and which might be so called, not properly, but in a *pretty, fanciful* way—because it was crowned with a death of martyrdom! The apostle then, through six mortal chapters, has been hammering at a rough, uncouth figure, and the result of all his learned labor is—absolutely nothing! Nowhere, in all the annals of writing, can be found an instance to compare with it, of the "montes parturiunt, nascetur ridiculus mus." It would be idle to allege the context against such expounders. They grant every thing we say concerning its entire and perfect harmony with the doctrine of vicarious satisfaction: all they ask us to allow, is, that the whole book may be a metaphor run mad. We would rather doubt the sanity of some of its expositors.

These examples may suffice of the advantage derived from studying the context. It is unhappily much discouraged and impeded by the way in which our modern Bibles are printed. The fracture of great coherent masses into verses, is an unhappy arrangement. The reader's attention is almost necessarily carried away from the flow and current of thought, and fixed on an isolated proposition, whose true meaning depends upon something not distinctly before his mind: in consequence, he is very apt to treat revelation as an immense collection of proverbs; and the majority of common readers actually so consider it.

The custom of reading the New Testament in this manner, originated with Robert Stephens the famous printer, who having published editions of it which met with great acceptance, determined to add a Concordance: and for convenience of reference, chopped the text into its present form; making it resemble more an auction catalogue, than a civilized-christian book. His son Henry states, that he went through the whole business while on horseback, (in equitando) which we are quite disposed to believe, as the exercise was well adapted to shake out verses without straining violently the reader's intellect. The mischief which it has caused in relation to the study of scripture, is far greater than those suppose, who have never reflected on the subject. How ridiculous would a modern letter appear, ex. gr. Washington's Farewell Address, if mutilated in this savage manner! Yet such is the effect of custom, that it scarcely excites notice, when performed on a writer who least of all can bear such an infliction—the rapid, discursive and exuberant Paul.

Nor can we approve the practice adopted by many preachers, of running into their pulpits with a single sentence or part of one, which they make their exclusive subject; not bestowing on the connection a word of notice—unless they have been hurried in their preparations, and find it convenient to talk a little *round it*, in an extempore introduction. What would we think if we heard any other book prelected on in this way—a treatise on medicine for instance, or on morals: or what would we think of a judge expounding in this way a legal statute? The civil law has laid down an express canon on the subject, with some tartness, as if indignant at the idea of such a practice: "*Turpe est* de lege judicare, tota lege non inspecta."

Ministers are often heard to chide their people sharply, for the careless and unprofitable way in which they read the word of God : but they would do well to ask, whether they are not themselves to blame in forming them to such wretched habits of perusing it. When his Reverence appears before the people month after month, without in a single instance perhaps, explaining the design, coherence, and argument of a paragraph containing only six verses, it is really too much to expect, that honest John will spend his Sabbath evenings in supplying the pastor's lack of service.

The same evil prevails in the domain of controversial theology. Many allow themselves to be captivated by the mere sound of a phrase. It seems to suit their purpose in an argument: incontinently they detach it from the paragraph to which it belongs, dress it up in high-sounding paraphrase, and send it forth, "to root out, pull down and destroy" every thing that opposes. Examples without number could be given, from the writings of all religious parties, even our own, for that many passages which Calvinists quote are utterly irrelevant, the slightest examination shows. An instance of this is the celebrated declaration in Jeremiah xxxi. 3: "I have loved thee with everlasting love, therefore with loving kindness have I drawn thee," which may be more properly translated thus,

> In days of old have I loved thee,
> Therefore will I prolong my goodness to thee.

God is here assuring the ten tribes of deliverance and protection, on account of the love he bore them in former times, when with outstretched arm he brought them from the land of Egypt. Nothing is said of the eternity of his purposes, or their accomplishment in the conversion of the elect: if applied to this subject, it must be in the way of pious accommodation. The same is true of another favorite passage: Matthew xxii. 14, "Many are called, but few are chosen." The whole context and scope shows, that the Redeemer is not speaking of sovereign election, but rather stating the fact, that while all are invited to the Gospel feast, there are comparatively few *admitted*, in consequence of neglecting to secure the necessary qualifications.

On the other hand, our Arminian brethren quote, with as little shadow of reason, 1 Corinthians, xii. 7, to prove universal grace. The proposition that "a dispensation of the spirit is given to every man to profit withal," sounds indeed bravely. But the sound is all: the whole argument shows that the Apostle is speaking of supernatural gifts of the spirit, and is addressing church members exclusively.

When we apply our Rule to interpretation, some caution is necessary, in consequence of the context being occasionally broken by a parenthesis. In the New Testament these are very frequent, especially with Paul, whose impetuous genius often starts aside to embody a vivid conception or glowing sentiment that suddenly kindled in his mind, and which he did not allow himself leisure, to weave into the general texture of his discourse. We have a beautiful example in 2 Timothy, i. 16, 18: where the short prayer in the beginning of the 18th verse is evidently an extempore burst of grateful emotion, and the words must be enclosed in brackets: "But when Onesiphorus was in Rome, he sought me out very diligently and found me, (*the Lord grant unto him that he may find mercy of the Lord in that day,*) and in how many things he ministered to me at Ephesus, thou knowest very well." A more striking instance is in Ephesians iii. where the first and fourteenth verses must be immediately united, the parenthesis consisting of not less than thirteen.

Attention to this, wonderfully enlightens some of his dark sayings; among others, that in 1 Timothy, v. 23: "Drink no longer water, but use a little wine for thy stomach's sake and thine often infirmities." The Apostle is in the midst of a solemn and weighty exhortation to Timothy, in relation to ordaining candidates for the ministry. In the 22d verse, he says, "lay hands suddenly on no man, neither be partaker of other men's sins, keep thyself pure." In the 24th he carries out the thought, stating that some men's disqualifications were open and manifest to all, others were more secret and followed after them. There is thus a complete connection between the 22d and 24th verses; and the question rises, how the Apostle comes to press the matter of wine-drinking directly between the two, when the thought was so foreign to his whole subject? It is manifestly a parenthesis. In the midst of his directions concerning ordination, he remembers that his young friend was of feeble constitution, and liable to severe attacks of dyspepsia. It is in his mind to prescribe a glass—not of syrup, but of good generous wine, which is known to possess great virtue in such complaints. No sooner thought, than done. Without losing a moment, he tosses it into the middle of his argument, where it stands a fine specimen of the noble artlessness of the great Apostle. Dr. Paley builds on this circumstance a strong argument for the authenticity of the epistle. It scarcely would have entered the mind of an impostor, to exhibit Paul as commending wine, in a grave, apostolical epistle: much less, would he have introduced the advice in so strange and improbable a manner.

RULE V.

We must know the character, age, sect, nation, and other peculiarities of the writer. Every human being has a *character*—a certain something which distinguishes him from others, giving a hue to all his thoughts and modes of expressing them. This must be known, in order to his being understood. The inspired writers are no exception to the rule. They who imagine that the Holy Spirit so possessed their minds that they became mere automata in his hands, and poured out words and thoughts as they were successively poured in—like so many water-pipes of a cistern, betray profound ignorance of the subject. Some such crude fancies were entertained in former times, and are probably not extinct. They doubtless originated in a vague notion, that the more entirely human agency was excluded from the doctrine of inspiration, the higher honor was bestowed on the Divine Spirit: and the etymology of the word "inspiration" had also its effect. It originally and properly signified, a *breathing in*, and suggested the dark and mysterious conception of an effect produced on the thinking substance of a man, not unlike the inflation of a bladder—

> "magnam cui mentem animumque,
> Delius inspirat vates."

But inspiration has nothing in common with its etymology: it simply expresses the idea of supernatural assistance and guidance, in the communication to mankind of truths previously unknown. Those who were honored with it, were enabled to speak, act and write, as divine messengers, in perfect conformity with the will of Him who sent them; so that nothing proceeded from them, but what was holy and true. Yet they were not puppets, acted on by a physical and compelling force from without. They were living, personal agents, in full possession of all the faculties with which they had been endowed by their Creator—with perception, memory, consciousness, will; and the energy of the Holy Ghost wrought no greater violence on their minds in the exercise of these powers, than is wrought by his ordinary operation on the hearts of believers in every age of the church.

It is not our business to give the philosophy of this "pre-established harmony" between agencies so different, nor to speculate on the mode in which they were combined for the production of a single result. As interpreters, we *state* the fact—not *explain* it: and the fact certainly is, that no men are more distinguished from each other by strong mental idiosyncrasies, nor any who give more decided evidence, that their own spirits performed an important office in composition. In the author of the book of Proverbs, we see before us the grave, sententious, dignified monarch, whose profound knowledge of human nature, and sparkling gems of wisdom, made his name celebrated throughout the East. Amos is always the strong, bold, but somewhat unpolished herdsman of Tekoah. The rough and vehement Ezekiel, standing with dishevelled hair and rolling eye, in the midst of his fantastic but expressive symbols, never suffers us to mistake him for Isaiah, the sublime, imaginative, tasteful courtier of Hezekiah. The same with the plaintive, tender Jeremiah—the contemplative John—the argumentative, glowing Paul. It is an old, but, with proper explanation, perfectly true remark, originally made by Jerome, that "revelation consists in thought, not in words or external dress: nec putemus in verbis scripturam evangelii esse, sed in sensu." We insult the Holy Ghost, by supposing him unable to accommodate himself to the mode of thinking and phraseology of those whom he honored with his influence—that when he made the prophet, he was forced to unmake the man.

When we read the Epistle to the Romans therefore, we must remember that we are conversing with a finished gentleman of the old school; a scholar brought up at the feet of Gamaliel, a powerful but a rapid reasoner, delighting in ellipses, digressions, repetitions, bold figures, and pregnant expressions suggesting more than meets the ear—fond of illustrating his subject by Old Testament ideas, even when he intends making no use of them in argument; and above all, that we are conversing with him who, more than any other apostle, was deeply penetrated with the glorious catholicity and abounding grace of the Gospel! In reading James, we must think of the stern, high-souled moralist, in whom the ethical element of Christianity seems to have taken the deepest root; who, while with adoring faith he beheld "the Lamb slain from the foundation of the world," never lost from his view the awful form of that "eternal law," which spoke in thunder from Sinai, and yet speaks in milder tones, though with the same commanding authority, to every child of Adam. John, in his writings, seems to be still clinging to his master's bosom.—Love to the person of his Redeemer is evidently his engrossing sentiment. No one can doubt, apart from every argument containing in other parts of Scripture, that John believed him to be divine. His glory as the uncreated Logos—that glory which he had with the Father before the world was, a few scattered rays of which had been seen through the veil of his humiliation, is the great thought with which his soul holds constant communion, raised above every other object—like the eagle calmly reposing in mid heaven, and *gazing at the sun!* He who gives no attention to these things, and does not take pains to catch the distinctive peculiarities of the sacred writers, commits the same kind of blunder with that of the man who reads Milton's Paradise Lost, and Addison's Essays in the Spectator, yet sees no difference between them except in the length of the lines.

• It is important also, to note the different kinds of composition they employed. Some were poets, and must be interpreted according to the laws of poetry. Their bold tropes must not be turned into sober matter-of-fact realities; as is done by the Millenarians, who read Isaiah nearly as they would Blackstone's Commentaries on the British Constitution. Ezekiel is not Luke, nor is Matthew the publican, David, singing one of the sweet odes of Zion to the music of his harp. Historians are to be treated as historians, not as poets or rhetoricians: the accounts of miracles given in our four Gospels, must therefore be taken to the letter. No books in the world bear more decided evidence, that their authors intended to give simple and perspicuous narratives of events as they actually occurred. The principle must not be tolerated for a moment, of explaining them away, by doing violence to the plain meaning of language, and to all the laws which are applied to other historical compositions. Yet it has been sanctioned by great names, especially in Germany. Grave divines are found, who insist that there is not one miracle in the Gospels; the events which *seem* miraculous being entirely natural, but exaggerated and embellished, by the warm fancies of the people among whom they occurred. Only strip, they say, the Evangelists of this semi-poetic drapery, and the business of exposition will go on delightfully. Moses fares, if possible, still worse; as they turn him into an allegorist or reciter of mythological fables. The first ten chapters of Genesis contain about as large a body of real truth, as can pass without inconvenience through the eye of a needle—being made up of old stories and scraps of song, which mean nothing, or anything, that a lively fancy may suggest.

Let not the Christian student take great pains to refute this wretched infidelity, which does not openly avow itself infidel, merely because its advocates earn their bread by a profession of Christianity; the most of them, being either professors of Christian theology, or pastors of Christian churches. Indignandum de isto; non disputandum est. Such interpretations do not deserve the name. They are feats of jugglery and legerdemain; and their authors are conceited sciolists, who, pranking themselves as the high-priests of philosophy, prove by their irreverence for things sacred, that they have not reached the portico of her temple. The true philosopher always trembles, when he stands, or even suspects that he stands, in the presence of God! He cannot trifle with such a book as the Bible! He cannot sport with a volume, the falsehood of which, if proved, turns him over to the beasts, and deprives him of his last stake, as a candidate for the glories of immortality.

RULE VI.

In expounding Scripture, *let there be a constant appeal to the tribunal of common sense.* Language is not the invention of metaphysicians, or convocations of the wise and learned. It is the common blessing of mankind, framed for their mutual advantage in their intercourse with each other. Its laws therefore, are popular, not philosophical—being founded on the general laws of thought which govern the whole mass of mind in the community. Now, however men may differ from each other, there are certain universal notions, plain and obvious principles of knowledge, according to which speech is regulated:

when we try a work by these, we bring it to the standard of "common sense."

There is occasion for it every moment. Scarcely will we hear in a long and serious conversation between the best speakers, a sentence which does not need some modification or limitation, in order that we may not attribute to it more or less than was intended. Nor is the operation at all difficult. We make the correction instantly, with so little cost of thought, that we would be tempted to call it instinct, if we did not know that many of our perceptions which seem intuitive, are the work of habit and education. It would be an exceedingly strange thing, if the Bible, the most popular of all books, composed by men for the most part taken from the multitude, addressed to all, and on subjects equally interesting to all, were found written in language to be interpreted on different principles. But, in point of fact, it is not. Its style is eminently, and to a remarkable degree, that which we would expect to find in a volume designed by its gracious Author to be the *people's book*—abounding in all those kinds of inaccuracy which are sprinkled through ordinary discourse, hyperboles, enallages, and loose catechrestical expressions, whose meaning no one mistakes, though their deviation from *plumb*, occasionally makes the small critic sad. In such cases, we reject everything incompatible with evident truth; assuming that the Bible could never intend to contradict our reason, or teach in any possible case that two and two are five. We shall give a few illustrations.

1st. *It never teaches doctrines refuted by the testimony of the senses.* Thus, when David says that "he is poured out like water, and all his bones are out of joint, that his heart is melted in the midst of his bowels," we perceive instantly, that a literal pouring out and melting cannot be meant, as nothing of the kind has been ever witnessed. When the Redeemer, in the institution of the Supper, declares of the bread, that it is his body; and of the wine, that it is his blood, we necessarily understand him to be speaking figuratively and symbolically. My senses distinctly see, taste, smell, and feel, that the sacramental elements are nothing but real bread and wine. If the Scriptures really taught the popish doctrine of transubstantiation, they would declare a falsehood, which would be quite sufficient by itself to destroy their authority. The principle of believing a doctrine in direct opposition to the clear evidence of the senses, is destructive of all evidence. If my senses may deceive me, how shall I convince myself that I ever saw a book called the Bible, or read it, or ever heard of such a being as Jesus Christ? The delusion practised on me at the Lord's table, where I am eating and drinking the real body and blood of a dead man, while tasting and smelling bread and wine, may be part of a most extensive scheme of imposture, to which no limits can be assigned.

2d. Its statements *must be compared with the results of experience, and observation.* No one who reads the command, "Be perfect, even as your Father in heaven is perfect," with reference at the same time to the state of the world in all ages, can deny that it is to be taken with a grain of allowance. Let us *aim* at perfection, but not dream of attaining it—experience amply proving that there is no man who sinneth not. In Matthew x. 34, Christ tells his disciples, that "he came not to send peace on earth but a sword." History is the best commentary on this somewhat harsh expression. The Gospel occasioned discords in families and nations, by inducing some to accept its guidance, while others rejected it: these frequently led to persecutions, which were the sword alluded to in the text.

3. Passages must be *harmonized with established facts in science.* Truth is always in accordance with herself. Her two great books, Nature and Revelation, cannot be at variance, though the latter seldom trims her phraseology into conformity with the starched definitions of science; for which every man of taste and discernment likes her the better. The expressions therefore which represent the earth as at *rest*—as being *built on the waters*—as having *bounds and limits*—and the sun as *moving round it*, are not to be brought in collision with astronomy. The representations of God as *coming* to a place—*deserting* it—*asking questions*—*grieving*—*repenting*, must be explained

consistently with the first elements of natural religion, which teach that he is a pure Spirit, omnipresent, all-knowing, and above all change or perturbation. Lactantius, a Latin Father, must have lost his compass entirely, when he undertook to prove from the Scriptures, that God has passions—thus contradicting a plain and evident principle of reason.

Whether the sacred interpreter will be required to modify the old expositions of the first twenty verses of the first chapter of Genesis, in conformity with the decisions of Geology, is in the advanced and advancing state of that science, not difficult to answer. The proof of our earth having existed long before the creation of man, and of a succession of mighty changes having occurred which required ages to their completion, rests on so many well established facts, that it would be sheer folly and absurdity to deny the conclusion—especially, when the passage admits of no less than two constructions, in perfect harmony with it. God never inspired men to teach their fellow men the arts and sciences, nor did he ever furnish those whom he inspired for other purposes, with a single scientific fact above the level of their age. Their mission was to impart moral and religious truth: in all other respects they thought with the vulgar, and with the vulgar they spake. Had it been otherwise, Religion would have suffered a calamity, instead of gaining a vantage ground. It would have lost its virgin sanctity and elevation above the smoke and stir of earthly pursuits; it would have been mixed up with the endless revolutions and vicissitudes, which science ha experienced in different ages; and the human mind chained down to a blind unreasoning faith, would have lost every motive to the vigorous exertion of its excellent and almost divine faculties. Nor is this all. Had the ideas of the sacred writers been in advance of those entertained by their contemporaries, they would not have been understood—or if understood, excited only wonder and ridicule; in which case, scant favor would have been shown to their higher revelations.

Happily, they are relieved from all responsibility by the wise arrangement, which has committed the book of creation into the hands of other servants. Men of science (if it be *true* science) are the *apostles of nature;* whose announcements are entitled to the same confidence, which we profess toward the apostles of grace. The expression is not too strong. We affirm that the truths daily elicited by the crucible, the telescope, and the air-pump, the galvanic pile, and the geologist's hammer, are perfectly independent of anything laid down in the Bible; and must not be sacrificed to any pretended necessity of giving it a meaning, at variance with these truths. If Paul were on earth, and asserted that water was a simple and homogeneous substance, we should not believe him, though he accompanied his assertion with a miracle—because no miracle would be so great as that which he requires us to believe; viz. that a substance is simple, which the chemist has proved to be a compound, by actually reducing it to its elements and forming it out of them, *before our eyes!* Nothing then can be more ill-judged, than taking advantage of a few artless expressions of the sacred writers, so redolent of their simple age, and entirely beyond the circle of their inspired ideas, to raise the hue and cry of "infidelity," against those, who independently of scripture but with unfeigned respect for its religious authority, pursue their inquiries into nature. Nothing also is more mischievous; for it generates the very infidelity, which excites so much apparent alarm.

Great allowance however, should be made for our venerable order. The important and spiritual duties of our calling allow little time for excursions into other men's fields of labor; and consequently, in secular branches of knowledge, we are apt to be found lagging behind the age. Now it is extremely difficult for such, to feel the whole force of a scientific statement. We may yawningly admit it: but the belief is not a *necessity*, and a *fate*, to which we submit as to the great law of death. Hence, when the announcement seems to oppose some of our time-hallowed prejudices, we refuse all compromise; and proceed to denounce it with the thundering energy of a man, who who has detected a black conspiracy to rob him of his Bible. The remedy to this can be given in two words: *more light!* Nothing dissipates panic terrors, like acquaintance with the cause—as experience proves in other cases. "Lead him," says an admirable little recipe which we have read somewhere, "close to the object, taking off his blinkers. If he starts, and throws back his ears, pat him and speak kindly: make him steadily look at it—leading him round and round. In a short time he will understand the thing, become as gentle as a lamb, and give you no farther trouble."

4. The Bible *cannot be at issue with any of our intuitive moral judgments.* If it recommends the "cutting off a right hand and plucking out a right eye," it must not be taken to mean bodily mutilation. Our life and members are a sacred trust committed to us, which we dare not trifle with. When Christ says, "If any man hate not his father and mother and wife and children, he cannot be my disciple," he is using a strong hyperbole, to denote the greater love which we should bear himself. Our moral sense revolts at the idea of hatred to parents, and no exposition can be tolerated, that would sanction a feeling so detestable. In Luke x. 4, he commands his disciples "not to salute (during one of their missionary journeys) any by the way,"—a precept which our Quaker Brethren obey to the letter. But Christ could never have intended to inculcate rudeness; it must therefore mean, "Do not lose time by holding unnecessary intercourse with your friends; use all expedition in journeying to the scene of your labors." Equally absurd is their well known exposition of the precept, "When smitten on the one

cheek, turn the other also;" as if the Saviour disapproved of self-defence.

On a similar principle, we explain those passages, which exhibit the prophets as doing by command of God, things inconsistent with natural propriety. Hosea, for example, is commanded to marry two impure women; Ezekiel to lie on his left side a year and a month, looking at an iron pan—then turn over to his right side, on which he must lie forty additional days—eating during the whole period a compost of lentiles, beans, barley, millet and fitches, prepared in a manner most decidedly disagreeable. We affirm boldly, that the expositors who consider these and others which might be mentioned, as real transactions, dishonor the word of God, while they betray a want of taste that is astounding. Beyond all doubt, they were symbolical representations, that passed before the Prophet's mind in his inspired ecstasy.

The rule under our notice, requiring us to try expressions by the standard of common sense, is of great use in explaining a class of propositions very frequent in Scripture, which seem to have no limit in their application, but must be restricted by the mind of the reader. They are thrown out by the writer, with the noble carelessness of one who takes a strong view of a subject, and determines to strike with it—not caring for the great swarm of little *buts*, that invariably rise before the mind of a feeble thinker, and darken the principal idea. We shall add a few examples.

Absolute expressions, often denote only what *usually* takes place. Solomon tells us in Proverbs xxii. 6, "train up a child in the way he should go, and when he is old he will not depart from it." This is not always true: Odd as it may seem, Solomon himself was an exception. Yet it is true generally: a wise and pious education gives good reason to expect the divine blessing. Sometimes they only denote the *tendency* of a thing. Proverbs xv. 1, "a soft answer turneth away wrath." It is calculated to produce this happy effect. Paul declares, that the "goodness of God leadeth to repentance." With submission to the Apostle—not always. Too often, it corrupts and hardens.

At other times, they only indicate *duty—right—official obligation.* Thus Solomon says, Proverbs xvi. 10, "a divine sentence is in the lips of the king, his mouth transgresseth not in judgment." Peter, in like manner says of the civil magistrate, "he is the minister of God for good, a terror to evil workers and a praise to them that do well." Such declarations show what he is *de jure:* the *de facto*, is quite another question, as Peter himself experienced shortly after; being put to death by one of these divine ministers in the most cruel manner. The same principle we apply to those statements which exhibit the Redeemer as dying for "all"—for "every man"—for the "sins of the world." They contain a precious charter of privilege—right—and consequent obligation to accept him. He is by office the *world's saviour:* all may enjoy the blessings which he hath purchased, and are excluded simply by unbelief.

Occasionally, we find assertions broadly made that refer only to *external character* and profession. Paul describes apostates as counting "the blood of the covenant wherewith they were sanctified, an unholy thing." They were so in *appearance.* Having avowed their attachment before the church and the world, they were recognized as true disciples and heirs of the promise. Yet of such, another Apostle declares, "they went out from us because they were not of us: for if they had been of us, they never would have departed." So, all credible professors are called "saints" and "holy." The sacred writers always treat them as being what they ought to be. This practice of naming things from their appearance is quite common. The impostor Hananiah for instance, is called in Jeremiah xxviii. 1, a "Prophet." False pretenders to piety, are in Matthew ix. 13, called righteous: "I am not come to call the righteous but sinners to repentance." Paul in 1 Corinthians i. 21, names the preaching of the Gospel "foolishness," because it was thought such by the haughty Greek.

There are other ways in which propositions stated absolutely, must be limited. Indeed, so various are they, that no definite rule can be laid down which will apply to every case: each should receive the modification dictated by common sense. The precept for instance, requiring us "not to revenge ourselves," forbids the taking private vengeance, not judicial punishment. Christ, in Matt. v. 33, commands us to "swear not." The connection shows us, that he refers to unnecessary and extrajudicial oaths; but independently of arguments from the context, we might safely assume that he never could have intended to nullify an institution almost coeval with the human race, and which he sanctioned by personal example. We are commanded in like manner, to "take no thought for the morrow"—to "judge not, that we be not judged"—to "pray without ceasing"—expressions which it is scarcely possible to misunderstand—though it would not be safe to stake much on the assertion; many betraying a perversity of thinking where Scripture is concerned, that on any other subject would be ludicrous. The Wrongheads in theology are still a numerous generation, though we hope decreasing.

RULE VII.

Study attentively the tropes and figures of the sacred writings. These are deviations from natural simplicity of expression; one idea being substituted for another, and made to represent it on the ground of some relation between them; as when I call a warrior, a lion; compare the march of an undisciplined army, to the flight of a noisy flock of cranes, or address a dead or absent person as if possessing life. They abound in all languages, and in many instances are the very language of nature. The least excitement of feeling impels a man of ordinary fancy to express his thought, not by the word directly appropriated to it, but by some accessory idea, which he prefers on account of its greater vivacity and beauty. Thus, old age is the *evening* of life; youth the *morning;* error is *blindness;* a great statesman, the *pillar* of the commonwealth. The fields *smile*—the stones *cry out*—the heavens *weep*. No one fails to perceive the superior liveliness and brilliancy of such modes of expression.

Nor will their frequent occurrence in the Bible surprise us, when we consider that much of it is poetry, and its birth-place the imaginative East. Its figures are not only numerous but exceediugly bold—sometimes even startling to an occidental ear and a taste formed on classic models. "The blood of Abel cries from the ground." "God makes drunk his arrows with blood." "The heavens celebrate the praises of Jehovah." "The floods clap their hands." "When Israel came out of Egypt, the sea saw it and fled, Jordan was driven back, the mountains skipped like rams and the little hills like lambs." Such is the glowing language that meets us in every page, and justifies the remark that it is by far the richest volume of fancy in our literature. The tropes which occur most frequently, are the following:—

1. Metonymy. This denotes the *substitution of one word for another, where the thoughts are closely conjoined* and rise up together in the mind, though there be no proper resemblance between them. Such are the ideas of cause and effect—subject and attribute—container and contained—sign and thing signified.

The *cause is put for the effect.* Thus the Holy Spirit is put for the gifts and influence of the Spirit. 1 Thess. v. 19, "quench not the Spirit." Luke xi. 13, "how much more shall your heavenly Father give the Holy Spirit to them that ask him." Rev. i. 10, "I was in spirit on the Lord's day, i. e. a state of mind caused by the Spirit. In the same sense Jesus was "led by the spirit into the wilderness to be tempted of the devil:" he went there, under a divine prompting and impulse. Parents are sometimes put for their posterity, as Judah for the Jews; and in Ezek. xxxiv. 23, David is used for Messiah, his promised son and successor to his throne: "I will set up one shepherd over them, and he shall feed them, even *my servant David.*" Frequently the converse of our rule takes place—the effect being put for the cause. Christ is called "our life," because he is its author. "He is made of God unto us wisdom, righteousness, sanctification, and redemption:" i. e. God has constituted him the source of all those blessings. In Hebrews vi. 1, the Apostle calls sinful works "dead." In what sense are they dead? Some reply, because they have no moral principle or vitality in them: but this is too weak. They are probably so called, metonymically, because they lead to death. In Rom. vii. 7, Paul asks "is the law sin?" he means to inquire, whether it produces sin.

The container is put for the contained. A table, denotes the food placed on it: "Let their table become a snare." A cup stands for the liquor it contains: 1 Cor. x. 16, "The cup of blessing which we bless." Heaven, for God himself. Hence the often recurring phrase, "kingdom of heaven," applied to the new dispensation of Messiah. There is no direct allusion in it to the heavenly state, but simply to its divine origin: in other places it is expressly called the kingdom of God, Matt. xix. 24, Luke xiii. 29. *House*, signifies the *family* residing in it. Gen. vii. 1, "Enter thou and all thy house into the ark." This is its meaning in Ex. i. 21, which states, that because the "midwives feared God, he made them houses." If the idea of giving two midwives a pair of houses be a little odd, there is nothing strange in Divine Providence rewarding their kindness to the families of his people, by giving them large and flourishing families of their own. On this use of the word, Pædobaptists found one of their strongest arguments for infant baptism. It is contended, that the "houses" which the Apostles baptized, must have included all of the family, young as well as old—such being the way in which the term is uniformly employed.

The sign for the thing signified; as a sceptre or shepherd's staff for *power.* To "lift up the hand" is to *swear:* "to bow the knee" is to *do homage:* to "put on sackcloth" is to *mourn.* Baptism is by a like metonymy identified with the moral renovation which it symbolizes. The neglect of this figure led the ancient Fathers, who are followed by many in the present day, to hold that baptism was itself regeneration—founding their opinion on the words of Christ to Nicodemus, "except a man be born of water and the spirit, he cannot enter the kingdom of God;" and the language of Paul, Tit. iii. 5, "he saved us by the washing of regeneration and renewing of the Holy Ghost." From these expressions they infer, that a positive renewing grace is actually communicated to the subject of the ordinance, and with it a complete forgiveness of sin previously committed. Were we believers in this doctrine, we should spend a considerable part of our time in marvelling at the singular taste of the Apostle Paul, who declined administering baptism, except in a few extraordinary cases; and even thanks God that he had *regenerated* none but Crispus, Gaius, and the household of Stephanus, 1 Cor. i. 16. The same Apostle, however, in another place, expressly claims the honor of having begotten them, though he had no agency in their baptism; 1 Cor. iv. 15, "In Christ Jesus I have begotten you through the Gospel." Equally strange is it, that our blessed Lord should have declined to perform a rite, which, for the stupendous effects produced by it on the corrupt and darkened mind, infinitely surpassed all his miracles on the body! The doctrine seems, on other accounts also, really incredible; and we deem it far more reasonable to suppose, that moral renovation is coupled with baptism in the passages quoted above, because of the sacramental and symbolical relation between them. As in Acts vii. 8, circumcision is called the "Covenant," because it was the sign of the Covenant: so baptism is the "washing of regeneration," because it is the visible token of it, on the application of which, a man becomes accredited as a citizen of the great spiritual commonwealth, which Christ has washed in his blood.

Frequently, *a sentiment or action is used for the object with which it is conversant.* Faith signifies not the *belief*, but the *doctrine believed:* "Contend earnestly for the faith." Hope stands for Christ, the great *object of hope:* Col. i. 27, "Christ, the hope of glory." Desire, for the *thing desired:* Ezek. xxiv. 16, "Behold I take away the desire of thine eyes [the prophet's wife] with a stroke." Thus Christ may be called "the desire of the nations," on account of the earnest longing for a Saviour, and actual expectation of one about to appear, which preceded his advent. The passage in Haggai, however, where the expression is used, will hardly bear an immediate reference to the Messiah. The context, as well as certain grammatical considerations, prove that the treasures of the Gentiles are meant, which the prophet says shall be brought in great abundance to adorn the second temple. That the whole paragraph contains a prophecy of Christ is almost certain; but nothing of that kind is involved in this particular phrase.

2d. Synecdoche, is the *substitution of a whole for the part, or a part for the whole.* Of the first kind, the following are examples. "The "world," denotes sometimes the Roman Empire, which was a very small portion of it. "Augustus decreed that the whole world should be taxed." "All," is put for a single individual. Thus it is said of King Joash, that his servants slew him for the blood of the *sons* of Jehoida, the priest, 2 Chron. xxiv. 25. But it appears from the 20th verse, that Joash had killed but *one* son, the Prophet Zechariah. In Judges xii. 7, it is said that Jephtha was "buried in the cities of Gilead." He could be buried of course only in one. The neglect of this synecdoche led some Jewish commentators to invent the strange fable, that to punish him for the sacrifice of his daughter, his body was chopped into pieces, and a part interred in each of the principal cities.

Sometimes, *All* is equivalent to *Many.* "*All* Jerusalem went out to John the Baptist." The devil showed to our Redeemer "*all* the kingdoms of the earth and their glory." At others, it denotes *all kinds:* Acts x. 12. Peter saw a great sheet, "in which were [literally] *all* four-footed beasts of the field." Our translators have rendered the expression more intelligible, but in so doing forsaken the original, as they have done also in translating Matt. iv. 23; where the Greek says that Christ "healed all sickness and disease among the people." All *manner* of sickness, is undoubtedly the idea intended. On this synecdochical use of the word, those who contend that in no sense can Christ be said to die for the non-elect, found their explications of the numerous passages objected to their view. Nothing more is meant, they say, than that he died for "all kinds of men." Happily, these gentlemen are themselves a synecdoche—and, we trust, a small one—of the party to which they belong. Calvinism can boast of a different class of expositors, among whom is found Calvin himself—than whom few use stronger language, in describing the magnificent fulness and universality of the gracious provisions of the Gospel.

The part is put for the whole; as in Acts xxvii. 37, "There were in the ship two hundred souls." The soul here comprehends the entire man. Many, is substituted for all; Dan. xii. 2, "Many that sleep in the dust shall awake, some to everlasting life, and some to shame and everlasting contempt:" the prophet certainly does not mean to describe a partial resurrection in these remarkable words. Rom. v. 19, "By one man's disobedience many were made sinners:" who the many are, we find in the former verse: "By the offence of one, judgment came upon *all* men to condemnation." A striking example of the figure we have in Ex. xii. 40, which has given much trouble to critics: "Now the sojourning of the children of Israel, who dwelt in Egypt, was four hundred and thirty years." But it can easily be proved, that four hundred and thirty years include the entire period from the calling of Abraham out of Ur of the Chaldees: how then are the Israelites represented as dwelling during that whole period in Egypt? We answer, that the part is put for the whole—Egypt, for the entire region in which Abraham sojourned with his descendants. Being an important part, and that in which they resided last, the writer singles it out to represent all the other scenes of their pilgrimage. The whole thought is given by the Septuagint translators, who insert after Egypt, "*and in the land of Canaan.*"

On Synecdoches of this kind, is founded a general canon very useful to be remembered in exposition, viz: that Scripture often exhibits a general truth in the form of *a particular case*—not that it is the only one, but that it explains the principle, and suggests the mode of applying it to all others. The language and education of the writers indisposed them for dealing in abstractions: everything is definite and particular, and may be almost pictured to the eye. But we shall do them the grossest injustice, if we suppose they rested here. There was doubtless a great general idea distinctly before their mind, of which the picture was the symbolical representation. When the wise man in Prov. xx. 10, says, "Divers weights and divers measures are an abomination unto the Lord," who can doubt that he thought of the other innumerable frauds practised by shopkeepers on their customers? The Psalmist tells us, that "the good man is ever merciful and *lendeth*." Accommodating a poor and industrious man with a loan of money is true kindness, but not the only expression of it. Christ, in Matt. vi. 1, forbids us to do our alms before men;" he means that we should conceal, if possible, *all* our benevolent actions. In John xiii. 14, he says, "Ye ought to wash each other's feet:" he might equally have said, for it is what he intended, "Be humble and mutually affectionate."

In a like way, those who justify the practice of granting divorce for other causes than adultery, interpret the words of Christ in Matthew v. 32: "Whosoever shall put away his wife, save for the crime of fornication, causeth her to commit adultery, and whosoever shall marry her that is divorced, committeth adultery." The fornication here stated to be the only ground, they view as the *principal* one, standing for others equally serious, as desertion, violence, and continued ill-treatment. They contend, that the scope of the Redeemer is to attack the doctrine of *arbitrary divorce*, not to lay down in form the justificatory causes; and appeal to the parallel passages, Mark x. 4, Luke xvi. 18, which give the prohibition, without even specifying fornication as an exception. Why, they ask, should the statement of Matthew be considered a complete enumeration of the justifiable causes of divorce, when the other evangelists give none whatever? declaring, absolutely, "Whoso shall put away his wife, and marrieth another, committeth adultery?" May it not rather be viewed as a synecdochical expression of the thought, that no divorce is valid which is not founded on the *strongest reasons?* We think the argument of these gentlemen is exceedingly plausible, if not entirely satisfactory; and remember having so entirely convinced by it a worthy old friend, who paid daily visits with great fear and trembling to an equally worthy lady, divorced for causes not laid down in St. Matthew, that he came to the point at once, and rejoices when he hears the name of our figure mentioned.

We have a lingering doubt, whether the example just given be not somewhat strained. Our next is much more clear and certain. The principle we are illustrating, is of special use in explaining the Mosaic law, which some have degraded into a mere civil institute, enjoining nothing but overt acts and a routine of external observances. Nothing seems more evident than that in the great majority of cases, the legislator is giving *examples*, leaving the generalization to the understanding of those whom he addressed. Paul was decidedly of this opinion, as appears from his comment on the precept: "Thou shalt not muzzle the ox that treadeth out the corn." He contends, that

Moses designed it not so much for oxen as for *men*, teaching by it, that the laborer is worthy of his hire. Nor can it be reasonably doubted, that the command not to "seethe the kid in its mother's milk"—not to "plough with an ox and ass together"—not to "sow different seeds in the same ground," with a hundred others, must be explained on the same principle. The good old custom, therefore, of spiritualizing, or giving moral extent to the ten commandments, which some modern writers object to, is a sound one, and justified by all the laws of interpretation: the Redeemer has given a most beautiful example of it in his sermon on the mount. This subject is well worth the student's attention. A habit of generalizing, without straining or doing violence to Scripture—of rising from particulars to great catholic principles, which come home to every man's business and bosom, is one of the most valuable acquisitions he can make in his theological course.

3. Metaphor, is founded on *the resemblance between objects;* being the substitution of one thing for another, which is like it. When I say, "God is my protector," I express the thought in its simplicity: When I say, "He is my shield," I clothe it in metaphor. In no figure are the sacred oracles so rich as in this: but little need be said, as there is seldom any difficulty in explaining it. The great point to be remembered is, not to press the resemblance beyond the boundary intended by the author. When Christ de-

clares, that he will come as a thief, *suddenness of appearance*, not *wickedness of purpose* is the thought which he illustrates.

Anthropopatheia is reducible to this class, which exhibits the Divine Being, as clothed *with the attributes, and performing the actions of men.* Thus he has "eyes" and "ears"—and an "arm that is full of power." "His bowels are moved;" at his coming "the earth shook and trembled—he bowed the heavens and came down, and darkness was under his feet, and he did ride upon a cherub and did fly—the mountains saw him and quaked, the deep uttered his voice, and lifted up his hands on high." Occasionally, we find an accumulation of these images in one description, on which the poet expends the whole force of his genius. Some of these passages (called "*theophanies*" are awfully sublime—of which the 18th Psalm and the 3d chapter of Habakkuk may be quoted as specimens; the last of which, describing the appearance of God for the deliverance of his people, leaves behind it at a measureless distance, the loftiest strains of the classic lyre.

In explaining passages of an anthropopathic character, the rule is plain. They must be understood in a way suitable to the infinite majesty of God, and purged from everything savoring of impurity or imperfection. His "eye" is his infinite knowledge: his "arm," is his almighty power: the sounding of his bowels," is his tender love and compassion: his "repentance," is his purpose to change the course of his providence for good and sufficient reasons, springing out of moral conduct of his creatures: he is "angry," when he punishes the sinner; and his "fury," paints the severity of their doom.

The prevalence of this figure in scripture, has given occasion to much puerile declamation concerning the "rude and imperfect ideas entertained of God in early times"—as if the saints of the Old Testament really believed in the materiality of the Divine Being! The fancy deserves no refutation, as it is purely absurd. The truth is—*we* need the same expedient, however unwilling to own it, for imparting warmth and fixedness to our dim conceptions of the great and incomprehensible First Cause. They who maintain the contrary—who think that they can carry on their devotions without resorting to such "unphilosophical" methods of exciting emotion, are mistaken, and would give us a religion entirely unfit for human nature. Imagination must come to the aid of reason, and provide it with sensible ideas, to be a support to its feebleness. Perhaps, the whole of the magnificent scheme of our redemption rests on the anthropopathic idea—the incarnation of the eternal Son being a substantial, living *theophany*, intended to furnish the worshipper with a visible object, to which his contemplations may be directed, while he attempts to leap the immense abyss between him and the Creator. When without this aid and on mere rationalistic principles, he undertakes the work, how is he lost in the endeavor! He finds in a moment, that he has no wings for such a flight: his affections cannot go forth to clasp a cold and barren abstraction, and he exclaims, with a dreary feeling of perplexity, "O that I knew where I might find him, that I might go even to his seat!" But the Gospel steps in with its cheering revelations. Heaven opens—and an amiable man appears, seated on a throne, and yet looking down upon him with the tender regard of an elder brother who died for his sake. "It is my Saviour!" he exclaims—"it is my God!!" Hisimagination is at once delightfully excited. His scattered thoughts have something on which they can rally and concentre; faith becomes actual vision; and with all the feelings of a child, he can draw near to the heavenly Majesty—for he hears that Saviour's own declaration, "He who hath seen me, hath seen the Father." Let us be thankful that it is so—and bless our wise and merciful Parent that when he contrived a religion for us, he did not call in *feelosofers* to his council!

Prosopopœia, is another form of metaphor, in which human actions and life are ascribed to inanimate or irrational objects. Examples are very frequent, and some exceedingly beautiful: but they are all easily understood.

4. Allegory, is a figure in which *one thing is expressed, and another understood.* It may be defined a continued metaphor, or an image founded on resemblance, carried out into a variety of details, for the

purpose of inculcating some moral truth. Nathan's parable of the poor man and his ewe-lamb; the description of the vine in the 80th Psalm; Jotham's apologue of the election of a king by the trees, in the 6th of Judges, and Paul's representation of the members of the body in 1 Cor. xii. are fine examples. All the parables belong to this class. Their only peculiarity is, that they narrate a series of fictitious *events;* other allegories are *descriptive.* But this makes no difference in their nature, or the laws of interpreting them.

Allegories consist of two parts; the sensible image or similitude, as drawn out into a series of imaginary facts, which we may call the *shell:* and the doctrine of moral truth illustrated, which may be called the *kernel.* The latter, is of course, not expressed, being contained in the shell, which must be broken before we become its masters. Practice, however, and the exercise of a little common sense, makes the operation a very easy one. There is always something in the connection, or the occasion, or the accompanying remarks of the speaker, or the nature of the thing itself, which informs us what great thought is to be elucidated. There are two important rules which the interpreter must observe in relation to this figure.

1. *Never seek for it;* nor turn into allegory, what admits of being understood in a plain and obvious sense. The rage for discovering mystical significations in Scripture, is one of the worst diseases with

which a young student can be infected. It has led to that infinite multitude of *types*, which disfigure the writings of many otherwise excellent writers, and throw a darkness, that may be felt over the sermons of many of our preachers. A type is a person or thing in the Old Testament, supposed to prefigure a person or thing in the New. It is, therefore, a divinely appointed practical Allegory, and was designed to prepare the minds of those living in the Theocracy, for the farther developments of truth which should characterize the age of the Messiah. In this point of view, a wise and well arranged system of types was an admirable expedient. They illustrated, in a way peculiarly lively and picturesque, the great principles of moral government, which remained to be unfolded in the latter day; so that no shock should be given to the pious mind by their unexpected novelty. "Sacrifices," made the people familiar with the idea of substitution. The "mercy seat," on which the Divine throne was erected, yearly sprinkled with blood, was a speaking allegory, from which they could not but infer something that prepared them for the Christian doctrine of reconciliation. Their water lustrations suggested the necessities of moral renovation. The like may be said of typical persons. The royal David, assisted them to conceive of a great theocratic monarch, whose kingdom was to be "an everlasting kingdom, and of whose government there should be no end." The mysterious king of Salem, so abruptly introduced in patriarchal history, and so abruptly withdrawn, in whom the attributes of priesthood and royalty were so strangely combined, and to whom Abraham himself paid homage, was well calculated to arrest the reflecting spirit, and induce the suspicion at least, that a new order of things might arise, which would exhibit the august spectacle of a priest upon a throne. We need not suppose that they perceived the full significance of these symbolical representations. It is enough that they suggested great and important hints—*seeds of truth*, rather than truth itself, which after lying buried and torpid in the depths of the soul during the long winter of the ancient economy, quickened into glorious life, "when the time of the singing of birds was come, and the voice of the turtle was heard in their land."

If now the question is asked, how far the system may be carried out: we answer, so far as it pleases God, and no farther. It is his prerogative to institute ordinances for his church, and when he does, *he lets us know it.* If Samson be an appointed emblem of the Lord Jesus Christ, I am sure that I shall find it in the Old or New Testament; if they be silent on the point, all his strength shall not compel my assent. I have no talisman given me, with which I can go into the simple perspicuous narratives of the book of God, and by a presto passe, turn its men and women into types! To prove their existence, much more must be done, than to show that one object on some points resembles another. Mere similitude may qualify for office, but cannot possibly induct into it; else Capt. Fluellen's celebrated theory of a typical connection between Alexander the Great, and king Harry of Monmouth, would be strictly true, being based on indubitable facts: 1st, that the birth-place of both commenced with an M.; 2d, that both were great fighters; and 3d, that there was a river in Monmouth and also a river in Macedon, though the honest gentleman had forgotten its name. The great point to be established, is, that the likeness was designed in the original institution. It is the *previous purpose* and *intention*, which constitute the whole relation of type and antitype. Now this must be proved, and there is only one way of doing it: show me from Scripture the existence of such a connection. Whatever persons or things in the Old Testament are asserted by Christ or his Apostles to have been designed prefigurations of persons or things in the New, I accept: but if you only presume the fact from a real or fancied analogy, you are drawing on your imagination, and assuming the dangerous liberty of speaking for God.

Nor is it enough to quote passages from the New Testament which refer to incidents in the Old. Many facts of the old economy are adduced simply as *happy illustrations*—to adorn or enliven a sentiment, not to prove it, of which we have no less than two instances in the second chapter of Matthew,—" The voice in

Rama, lamentation and great mourning—Rachel weeping for her children, and refusing to be comforted," spoken of by Jeremiah, was the mourning of the Jewish mothers when separated from their children on the way to Babylon. The Evangelist alludes to that catastrophe as resembling the murder of the infants by Herod, and says nothing more than that the one *illustrated* the other. This use of the phrase οπως πληρωθη is known to every scholar. "Any thing," as Dr. Bloomfield observes, "may be said to be fulfilled, if it admits of being appropriately applied." The quotation in the 15th verse, "out of Egypt have I called my son," is a like instance of accommodation. The departure of Israel from Egypt under Moses, of which Hosea speaks, Hos. xi. 1, was neither a prophecy nor type of the Redeemer's brief residence in that country. But there was a pleasing and interesting coincidence, which attracts the notice of the Evangelist, and induces him to borrow the prophet's words.

The consequence of neglecting these plain and rational principles, may be seen in the writings of divines without number. Large folios have been filled with types and antitypes, which exist only in the brains of their authors, the facility of the operation greatly recommending it to many. To become a good Grecian, and skilful collator of parallelisms, is labor indeed! Nothing more easy than to lie all day on a sofa, tracing likenesses between Delilah and Judas Iscariot—Adam's fig-leaves and the works of the law.

It is also very convenient; for each sect may provide itself with its own typology, from which, as from a fortress built in air, and therefore beyond the reach of human weapons, they may hurl defiance to every enemy. In this way, Pope Innocent the third proved to the Emperor of Constantinople, the immeasurable superiority of his Holiness to his Majesty. God, says he, made two great lights, i. e. he constituted two great dignities—the Papal and the Royal. The greater is the Papal, ruling in spirituals, or over the day: the lesser is the Royal, ruling in temporals, or over the night. From which it clearly follows, that as the sun is superior to the moon, so the Pope is exalted above Kings!

This was not bad. What his majesty replied we cannot say—though doubtless he contrived some method of turning the tables. The scheme, after all, in matters of argument at least, is not so convenient as we allowed it to be; as we can seldom bring the adversary to our own way of thinking about it, and our best cases may be so easily retorted. The types of theologians much resemble their little namesakes of the printing office, in one respect; however ingeniously set, one stroke of a mischievous elbow can dash them all into *pi*. Those who desire to see the way in which the subject is treated by some of our evangelical divines, may look into "McEwen on the Types." He is greatly commended by some; and we would not deny him the praise of lively fancy and sincere piety: but it is fancy run wild, and no degree of piety can give respectability to nonsense. We hold an interpretation not based on principles, to be an unprincipled interpretation, though endorsed by all the saints in the calendar. That there are persons and things in the ancient dispensation intended to be prefigurative of persons and things in the new, we have already expressed our belief. We go on solid grounds when we make the assertion, and appeal boldly in support of it to the "Word." But we will not desert that light for *ignes fatui*, or add our own muddy inventions to divine ordinances. The extravagances of the advocates of typology have done more to make the whole doctrine appear ridiculous than all the sneers and wit of infidelity.

Yet we would not be morose to our type loving brethren, nor refuse all compromise with them. That every question which arises must be decided by the word of God, is a point not to be surrendered, but whether direct and positive assertion is necessary, may be doubted. Even when nothing is said on the subject, the resemblance between two objects, whether persons or things, may be so striking—and so remarkable the coincidence of the attending circumstances, that a devout mind profoundly convinced of the initiatory and predictive character of the ancient œconomy, might be allowed to see in the correspondence something more than accident. Thus, without the express testimony of our Saviour, it might be conjectured (*perhaps*) that the exaltation of a brazen serpent on a pole darkly pointed to his own elevation on the cross : the resemblance being so close, and the expedients, adopted for healing the Israelites, being of so singular a character, that we are almost compelled to find some reason for it. So also had Melchisedec not been declared by the author of the Epistle to the Hebrews to be "made like unto the son of God," we might have guessed (*perhaps*) at something of the kind, from the abrupt and startling manner in which the book of Genesis introduces him on the scene, the union in his person of the sacerdotal and kingly offices, and the homage which he received from the father of the faithful.

Great care, however, as well as modesty must be exercised, when we expatiate in the agreeable but sterile field of conjecture. The navigator who forsakes his chart, in quest of new discoveries, should possess extraordinary skill and caution, for he is his own underwriter; he should also have an excellent temper, as his "valuable discoveries" often prove to be vexatious disappointments, turning on a near approach into —islands of ice—continents of fog—perchance, an archipelago of breakers. Facts might be adduced without travelling abroad, to prove that Hierophancy is far from being a harmless member of the *Fancy* family, but is often attended with serious danger. Walking among the shadows which his imagination has turned into living realities, the mystic seer is equally ready in the hour of reaction (for spite of every effort to the contrary, reflection will occasionally step in,) to turn realities into shadows, and thus make a total shipwreck of his religious faith and hope. We may rest assured of this, that the last man on earth to be relied on "for continuing in the faith grounded and settled," is the man so *full of faith*, that he sees its object everywhere and in everything. We advise, therefore, every interpreter to form habits of strict, nay severe, exposition of the sacred text ; let him always be content with what he can prove, and when the case is in the least dubious, prefer the *too little* to the *too much.*

2d. As we are not to seek for Allegory, so we must *consider only the parts which are connected with the doctrine taught*—paying no regard to external circumstances. Having mastered the scope of the writer, we must interpret so much of the figure as directly relates to it, and no more. The remark is of special use in explaining parables, though it applies also to types. The correspondence between them and the antitype, must never be pressed beyond the manifest design of God in establishing the relation. Levitical sacrifices prefigured the great atonement of the Redeemer; but we must not turn, as some have done, the tongs and fire-shovels of the altar into symbols. The High Priest typified the person of Christ; but it would be mere trifling, to discover profound meanings in every part of the sacerdotal dress. With regard to parables, the rule must never be lost sight of. Many circumstances in them are only added to give an air of probability, or render them more lively and interesting. They are (to use the beautiful expression of Solomon) "golden apples in silver baskets:" As interpreters, we have concern only with the *apples.* Circumstances, in short, form what may be called the machinery of the parable, and therefore do not always have weight in the investigation of its meaning.

The parable of the ten virgins for instance, is designed to teach the folly of those who neglect preparation for their Redeemer's coming. Virgins are selected, not on account of their purity, but because virgins in those days played an important part at bridals; and a bridal feast was made the basis of the fable. The virginity therefore of the personages is a mere circumstance, which teaches nothing. So is the distinction into "five wise," and "five foolish:" nothing can be inferred as to the comparative number of nominal and sincere professors of religion in the world. The two classes are equalized, to guard against all speculations on a subject foreign to the speaker's object. The "sleeping" of the wise virgins is another mere circumstance, introduced to bring about the catastrophe in a natural way—not to teach the dangerous doctrine that the best Christians fail in spiritual vigilance, and are very liable to be taken by surprise when the Master calls them. The truth is, that their sleeping was designed to be rather complimentary than otherwise, as it brought out the fact that they were *provided* and *ready*. They had nothing to fear: a little refreshment therefore was not amiss, especially as they had no duties to perform until the arrival of the procession.

The parable of the rich man and Lazarus, is another example. The angels who carry the soul of Lazarus to Abraham's bosom, probably belong, as well as Abraham's bosom itself, to the machinery, and nothing is deducible from it. The representation of the rich man and Abraham being in the same region, and within sight of each other, is an image taken from the ancient idea of Hades, and must not be called upon to prove, that the souls of the blessed hold intercourse with those of the wicked in another world.

Great prudence therefore, and good taste are needful, in explaining these interesting compositions. Without such qualifications, and foolishly ambitious of making every thing out of any thing, interpreters have often made them ridiculous. What can be more simple and intelligible than the parable of the good Samaritan, which so beautifully inculcates universal benevolence! It is absolutely transparent! Yet in the hands of some, it turns out a perfect riddle, where the true significance is not obscured, but utterly lost. The man whofell among thieves—is the *sinner;* the thieves, are the *devil and his angels;* the priest who passed by on the other side, is the *law;* the Levite, is *legal obedience*. The good Samaritan, is *Christ;*

the oil, is *grace;* the wine, comfort from the promises; the inn-keeper, is the Christian *Ministry ;* the coming again, is *death, judgment,* and *eternity.* All this may be very pious; but we repeat our maxim, that no piety can give respectability to nonsense.

RULE VIII.

Attend carefully to Hebrew, and Hebraistic idioms. In reading the Bible, never forget that its language, in every thing which distinguishes one from another, is at variance with your own. That this holds true of the language of the Old Testament, no one doubts; but the remark equally applies to that of the New. In its use of words, its grammar, and syntactical constructions, it has many of the peculiarities of its oriental sister; so that its authors may be said without much exaggeration, while they spoke in Greek to have thought in Hebrew. It could not be otherwise; an impure Hebrew being their native tongue, and their Greek style being formed by the constant reading of the Septuagint, which was an extremely literal translation of the Old Testament into that language. There is no reason to believe, that any of them except Paul, had ever read a single Greek author. The student should be mindful of this, and keep his Old Testament and Septuagint always before him. A few examples of the Hebraising style shall be given: details would fill a volume.

One striking instance, is the use of the Genitive, which has a much more extensive signification than is customary with us; comprehending a greater variety of relations; and often qualifying the noun which governs them as adjectives. This often occurs in the New Testament. In 1 Cor. i. 5, Paul says, the "sufferings of Christ abound in us." He means the sufferings not undergone by Christ, but which we undergo for him. Sufferings for the *sake* of Christ, would be the proper English expression. The same is meant by the Apostle, when he calls himself "a prisoner of Christ." He was a captive, on *account* of him. In various chapters of the Epistle to the Romans, he speaks of the righteousness of God, by which he plainly signifies, not the excellency of the divine nature, but the righgeousness by which the sinner is justified, and which he names "God's righteousness," because he graciously provided and accepts it. In the same way, "horn of salvation" signifies a horn (the emblem of power among the Hebrews borrowed from their pastoral life) which is the *cause of salvation;* in other words, (when stripped of its orientalism,) a mighty author of deliverance. The Hebrew mode of employing genitives for adjectives is also common. The Apostle addressing the Thessalonians, speaks of their "patience of hope," he means *patient hope.* "Glory of his power," is equal to *glorious power.*

The Hebrews were fond of giving emphasis to what they said, by repetition. Jer. xxii. 29, "Oh earth, earth, earth, hear the word of the Lord." Isa. vi. 3, "Holy, holy, holy, is the Lord God Almighty;" from which many have drawn a prodigiously silly argument for the Trinity.

Hendiadys is the *joining of two words by the copulative, while a single thing is asserted;* the one being generally employed as a genitive, or adjective: Acts xxiii. 6, "of the hope and resurrection of the dead I am called in question." This is a striking instance. He means the *hope of the resurrection* of the dead. In Acts xiv. 13, it is said that the "priests of Jupiter brought oxen and garlands to the gates." The garlands were upon the oxen: *crowned with garlands,* therefore, expresses the idea. Many judicious commentators explain by this peculiarity the phrase in Matt. iii. 11, "He shall baptize you with the Holy Ghost and with fire:" i. e. with *the burning Spirit*—with him who is powerful, penetrating, and all-purifying, as the element of fire.

There are singular examples of disregard to the regular construction of sentences in both the Old and New Testaments, which in a classical Greek writer would be offensive, but in our authors is positively agreeable; being so redolent of primitive simplicity. In Gal. iii. 4th, 5th, 6th verses, we have a series of propositions, which seem to defy all the efforts of interpreters to disembroil them.—Nothing is more common, than for the Apostle to commence a thought in a particular way, and conclude it in a manner entirely different, as if he had forgotten his beginning. Thus he commences the well-known comparison between Adam and Moses, in Rom. v. with the following sentence, or rather part of one, "Wherefore as by one man sin entered into the world, and death by sin, and so death passed upon all men, for all have sinned." He thus gives us reason to expect a redditive or corresponding clause to be introduced by the usual formula, "*so*," or "*thus*." None occurs; and after examining what follows, we are obliged to conclude that in the onward impetuosity of his movement, he has lost sight of his starting point—without however forgetting the thought, to which he does ample justice.

But it is *in the use of verbs*, that the Hebraism of Scripture appears most clearly. They very frequently express not the action itself, but something approaching or allied to it—the desire or endeavor to perform it—its commencement, or the giving occasion to it—its permission, or the obligation to its performance. We shall as usual give some examples.

Things are said to be done, where there is only *endeavor* or *desire*. Thus Reuben is said to "have delivered Joseph out of the hands of his brethren." He attempted his deliverance, but succeeded very partially.—"Whoso findeth his life," says our Redeemer, "shall lose it:" i. e. *seeks* to find it, is unduly anxious for its preservation.

Sometimes verbs only intimate that the subject *gave occasion* to the action. In Jeremiah xxxviii. 23, God says to King Zedekiah, "thou shalt be taken by the hand of the king of Babylon, and thou shalt cause Jerusalem to be burnt with fire." The conduct of the unhappy monarch should *lead* to this catastrophe. "The wrath of man," says the Psalmist, "shall praise God"—not praise him, but be an *occasion* of praise. This explains the apparent discrepancy between Matthew and Luke, in their account of the field of blood. The former states that it was bought by the priests and elders with the thirty pieces of silver, which Judas Iscariot had returned to them. The latter, in Acts i. 18, says, "this man (Judas) purchased a field with the reward of iniquity." The fact was, that he gave *occasion* for the transaction, and the historian describes him as the agent.

Frequently, words expressing the power of doing actions, only mean *facility;* and the denial of power signifies nothing more than *difficulty.* In Ruth iv. 6, the near kinsman of Elimelech says, "I cannot redeem his inheritance." He *could* have done it, for he was evidently a man of property, but not without considerable sacrifices. The householder in our Lord's parable, of whom a friend solicits admission at midnight, replies that "the door is shut, the children with him in bed, and that he *cannot* rise." He meant that rising was extremely inconvenient. So it is said of our Lord, in Mark vi. 5, that he could do no mighty works in a particular district, because of their unbelief: he could not with pleasure and satisfaction: it was painful to him to throw his pearls before such swine. The Pelagians appeal to this idiom, when they attempt to explain the sinner's inability to do what is good. He *cannot;* because in consequence of the strength of animal impulses, and of bad education, commencing at the mother's breast, it is extremely, and in the last degree, *difficult.* Their enlightened opponent meets them, not by ringing changes on the words "can," and "cannot," violently torn from their connection, but by a careful study of the passages in which they are found, directed by the laws of sound interpretation.

Words expressing actions, are often only *declaratory*—denoting the recognition of them as having been performed, or about to be.—"Behold," says Isaac to Esau, "I have made Jacob thy lord, and all his brethren have I given to him for servants." The only agency of the venerable patriarch in this transaction consisted in announcing it. He intended to say "I have *declared* Jacob thy lord." In a like manner, Jeremiah was set up by God "over the nations to root out, pull down, and destroy." The Prophet was not a military conqueror; but as a divine messenger, he declared what should be accomplished by the hand of Nebuchadnezzar. So also when the priest saw on a man signs of leprosy, he was ordered to "pollute or make him unclean," Levit. xiii. 3. The meaning is plain enough. He was to *pronounce* him unclean, as it is expressed in our English version, which very properly rejects the grosser Hebraisms.

The 7th verse of the 2d Psalm, receives great light from this declaratory use of verbs. "The Lord hath said unto me, thou art my son, this day have I begotten thee." Most of the old divines supposed that David is here describing the actual generation of the son from the father; having in thought carried himself back to a point in eternity when the generation was supposed to take place. The words "this day," refer to that imaginary point. The view cannot be sustained, and among other reasons for this, that though certain transcendental theologues of our times have invited themselves to be present at the generation —not only of the son, but the father from the great bosom of *Nichts;* nothing of the kind is found in sacred Scriptures. We do not believe that the most raging delirium could have made the pious, simple-hearted Psalmist imagine to himself a God *beginning to be*—or a God *half formed.* The word "begotten," is to be taken declaratively. The point of time assumed by the writer in this noble Messianic ode, is the resurrection of its subject from the dead. God is represented as addressing him on the occasion—presenting him to the admiring gaze of the whole moral universe; and acknowledging the endearing eternal relation of which, *on that day*, he had given such magnificent illustration. The clause may be thus briefly paraphrased: "Thou art my only begotten and eternal son. I here avow thee to be such, and require all my subjects to honor thee as a partner of my throne." With perfect propriety therefore, the Apostle connects the passage with our Lord's resurrection: Rom. i. 4, "declared to be the son of God with power by his resurrection from the dead."

The last example which we shall give, is of words signifying action, being used to denote the *permission of it;* as in the prayer of David, Psalm cxix. 31, "I have adhered to thy testimonies, put me not to shame." A more striking example we have in Isiah lxii. 17, "O Lord, why hast thou made us to err from thy ways, and hardened our heart from thy fear." In this passage and some others, the English reader is startled at discovering indications of the horrible doctrine, that God exercises a positive agency in the production of moral evil. Thus we are taught to pray, that he "may not lead us into temptation:" He "hardened Pharaoh's heart:" He "shuts the eyes of sinners, and makes their ears heavy, lest they see with their eyes and hear with their ears." They contain, however, nothing alarming; the whole doctrine which they teach, being approved by the light of reason itself; that God, in righteous judgment gives the presumptuous sinner up to his own evil impulses, permitting him to "harden himself, even under those means which he useth for the softening of others."*

* Westminster Confession of Faith.

Misapprehension of this idiom led many excellent men in New-England, to profess without scruple or limitation, their belief, that unholy volitions were the immediate effect of divine agency. The race is nearly extinct, having been succeeded (as might be expected from the usual course of things in the world), by a generation who seem afraid to trust the Supreme Being with any agency even in good. We have always reverenced those worthy men. We especially admire that iron intrepidity, which enabled them to look in the face and take to their bosoms so ugly a monster, from simple regard to the divine will. Men who could sacrifice to faith the strongest moral instincts of their nature, were prepared for anything. Yet after all—in the matter of expounding Scripture, *heroes* are of less account than good *hebræans.*

The student will be making small progress in the knowledge of his Bible, who does not soon find that we have been giving only a few specimens of its phraseology. Let him devote his best powers of attention to it; for there is not a tree in the garden which yields more precious fruit. What especially recommends it, is the fact, that in exploring the Hebraisms of the Bible, we go to the very fountain head of knowledge concerning the meaning of those important and constantly recurring words by which the New Testament writers describe the fundamental truths of Christianity; such as *faith, propitiation, redemption, atonement, church, baptism, regenera-*

tion, justification, and righteousness. Let a young man tolerably versed in the languages, sit down as ignorant as a babe of the Gospel, and study these words carefully as he finds them in his Hebrew and Greek Old Testament, with no other human aid but a good dictionary and concordance; we promise him with unbounded confidence, that he will obtain an infinitely clearer notion of them in a single week than by reading five hundred folios of polemic divinity.

RULE IX.

Much of Scripture being Prophetical, we should acquaint ourselves with the nature and laws of that kind of composition. This is far from easy. No department of theology has occasioned so much perplexity to serious inquirers, and the subject is still beset with difficulties, which we have little hope will soon be removed. God has suffered clouds and darkness to rest on it for the wisest reasons, some of which are obvious. He would not deprive his Church of the privilege which she has enjoyed in every age and place, of walking by faith. He would not by exhibiting a clear picture of the future, disturb the freedom of his creatures, and the natural course of human events: in short he would teach, that our religion provides other business for us, than to indulge a childish curiosity as to "times and seasons." We would not therefore encourage the student to speculate much on this subject. The predictions which have been fulfilled, especially those accomplished in the advent of our Redeemer, deserve all attention—being the strongest confirmation of the truth of our holy religion, and arguments of resistless force against the Infidel. As to futurity—let the "sapphire throne," borne by the flaming Cherubim, take its own mighty course. There is a "living Spirit in the wheels," who keeps his own counsel, and seems, if we may judge from the past success of Apocalyptic commentators, to treat with very little respect the numerous attempts to advise him. Scan as curiously as you will, the car of Providence in its magnificent progress through the earth: but choose wisely your post of observation, and by all means *mount up behind!*

The following hints on the general subject of Prophecy may be of use.

1st. *Remember, that the diction of this part of Scripture is intensely poetical.* Not only were its authors poets—in the common sense of the word, but in its richest and noblest acceptation. In splendor of imagination—in the gorgeous coloring which they throw over every thing they describe—in boldness of imagery and enthusiastic glow of feeling, they excel all other authors. How miserably such noble spirits will be explained by those who treat their productions as if they were discourses on History or Civil Government, we need not say. Quite as little may be expected from those, who discover in their writings a dark and tangled forest of hieroglyphics; insist that every image is a definite symbol of invariable signification; and actually turn the noblest creations of genius into an Egyptian alphabet, of which these great Champollions have been fortunate enough to discover the key that enables them to decipher the most crabbed page in the book of destiny!

2d. *They were while composing their predictions in a state of ecstacy or high supernatural excitement*, produced immediately by the inspiring Spirit. The influence they were under, we have reason to think, was of a much more engrossing and controlling character, than that which illuminated the minds of the Apostles. The latter, while they thought the thoughts and spoke the words of God, retained all their mental activity and self-command. Their ideas seem to have risen spontaneously, according to the laws of association, nor do we discover any traces of a compulsory necessity, in the election of some, and the rejection of others. No enlightened reader of Paul for instance, can doubt, that he *thought out* every thing he said, as fully as if he had not been under heavenly influence. His personality mingles itself in every sentiment he utters. He sends courteous salutation to private friends, describes his feelings on hearing favorable or painful accounts of them, reminds his young favorite Timothy of his ill health, speaks of a certain "cloak" which he had left at Troas, "as also the parchments," hopes to visit some of them, though he is not certain; nay, there are strong indications in one or two cases, of his concluding a letter, and then returning to it for the purpose of adding something new.

With the prophets it was different. They "were carried away," as the Apostle Peter expresses it, by the inspiring God, and seem rather to be acted on, than voluntary agents. Hence those various expressions which represent "the hand of the Lord as coming upon them," and their yielding to his influence as something involuntary on their part, accompanied with a feeling of horror and great darkness, and sometimes a falling to the ground: Gen. xv. 12; Num. xxiv. 4; 1 Sam. xix. 20. This is, of course, to be understood comparatively; for we have already observed, that even prophecy did not entirely paralyze reason and self-consciousness. But they were certainly wrought upon in a much more powerful manner, than the other holy men who were honored with a divine afflatus. Though not mere machines, nor agitated with a blind fury like the ancient Pythia of Delphos, they were yet not entirely themselves. The powers of perception and volition were for a time partially suspended, and their minds became so many placid mirrors, from which were reflected the pure rays of heavenly truth.

3d. In this state, *they saw objects as present to them.* The various incidents and transactions which were revealed, imprinted themselves vividly on their imaginations and with all the force of living truth, so that they possessed an ideal reality, similar to that which objects have in dreams. Hence the frequency with which they are called "Seers," and their revelations "visions." Thus Balaam, who was doubtless a true prophet, describes himself, as "the man whose eyes are opened, who heard the words of God, who saw the vision of the Almighty, having fallen upon the ground." Similar were the revelations of Isaiah: "In the year that king Uzziah died," he says, "*I saw* the Lord sitting upon a throne, high and lifted up, and his train filled the temple." On another occasion, *he sees*—a hero marching forward in splendid apparel, stained with the blood of conquered enemies, and exclaims in admiration, as if personally addressing him: "Who is this that cometh from Edom with died garments from Bozrah, that is glorious in his apparel, travelling in the greatness of his strength?" Ezekiel, when the hand of the Lord was on him, "*saw* and passed through a valley of dry bones," which, after being addressed by the prophet at the divine commandment, "came together, bone to bone, and the breath came into them, and they stood up an exceeding great army." Habakkuk stands upon his watch-tower, *to see*—what God will say and exhibit to him. These were not rare and isolated cases. They were of a more striking character than many, but they illustrate the general mode in which the prophetic mind was affected. In short, we may consider the future events predicted, as a large and magnificent *panorama*, encompassing the sacred visionary on every side, and becoming for a time his whole world of being, in which he breathes, and moves, as if in his proper home.

He did not, however, *see them in their strict relations to each other, nor in their chronological connection.* God did not think fit to exhibit a clear and perfect map, for wise reasons. Each saw pieces, *membra disjecta* of the mighty whole: but in no one place, do we find a prophet giving a symmetrical view of the entire compass of a subject. Sometimes, we find a rich delineation of the person of Christ; at others, a description of his kingdom and the glories of his reign. Here, note is taken of him, as meek, gentle, compassionate, who "will not break the bruised reed, nor quench the smoking flax." There, he is seen striking through kings in the day of his wrath, filling the places with dead bodies, and wounding the head over many countries. Some prophets, say not a word of his humiliation and cruel sufferings—Malachi for example. Only two, advert to his remarkable forerunner. Sometimes the vision is sad and melancholy, exhibiting the rejection of the Jews on account of their unbelief, and their utter dissolution as a people. At others, all is joy and sunshine. The city is rebuilt, the sanctuary is restored, all kings of the earth bring their treasures to it, and the ransomed of the Lord return with songs and everlasting joy upon their heads.

This *fragmentary* character of prophecy, is a very striking and important one. The want of duly considering it, is the principal cause of those complaints we often hear, especially from infidels, concerning the darkness of this part of revelation. Were such to sit down, and carefully unite the scattered pieces into a whole, they would be astonished to find how clearly, as well as fully and consistently, the Christian Saviour is delineated.

Equally deserving notice, is the fact, that they *seldom perceive objects as related to each other in time.* The reason has been already stated. They were in the midst of what they saw, like a man in a dream. The events of a far distant future were so many present realities, on which they gazed with terror or delight; unsuspicious, probably, that ages would elapse before the fulfilment. Thus Isaiah, chapter ix. 5, speaks of Messiah as if *already* born, and entering into his kingdom: "Unto us a child is born, unto us a Son is given, and his name is called Wonderful, Counsellor, the mighty God." In chapter xlii. 1, He directly points to him: "Behold my servant whom I uphold, mine elect in whom my soul delighteth." Instances of this are numberless. It is not surprising, therefore, that events most widely separated from each other, should be blended in prophetic description, and treated as continuous. They saw them *in clusters*—not in chronological succession.

Thus in the 10th chapter of Isaiah, we have a

thrilling account of the destruction of the Assyrians, which took place at least six centuries before the coming of Christ. Yet the prophet joins it immediately with that event, by the ordinary copulative: "*And* there shall come forth a rod out of the stem of Jesse, and a branch shall grow out of his roots." The conjunction of this great event with the return from Babylon, is so frequent, as to strike the most careless reader. Our Redeemer's prophecies display the same character. In the remarkable prediction contained in the 24th of Matthew, two great objects hovered before his mind: the destruction of Jerusalem, to take place in less than forty years; and his final coming in glory. Yet he passes from the former to the latter at once, and even intimates the succession by a word, (ευθεως,) which seems to exclude all interval or delay: verse 29; "*Immediately* after the tribulation of those days (the destruction of Jerusalem) shall the sign of the Son of man appear, and all the tribes of the earth shall wail, and they shall see the Son of man coming in the clouds of heaven with power and great glory, and he shall send his angels," &c. If any wonder that he should have conjoined two events so distinct from each other, by the strong adverb ευθεως; let him consider, that when our Redeemer assumed the prophet's mantle, he volunntarily placed himself under the prophet's laws. He saw objects, precisely as Isaiah would have done, and *spoke* as he *saw*.

This characteristic of the prophetic writings is inscribed on almost every page. All the Messianic passages exhibit it in a greater or less degree: many of them, for instance, placing the final consummation of all things in immediate juxtaposition with the first preaching of the Gospel. The field of sacred vision may, in this respect, be compared to a clear midnight sky. We see the stars above our head—star differing from star in magnitude and brightness, but their relative distance from us, or from each other, we are unable even to conjecture.

The subject may be illustrated by a fact in mental philosophy. It is now well understood, that sight gives no primary information concerning distance, in any case whatever. We obtain it from touch. Having acquired by the constant *handling* of objects, notions of their comparative nearness or remoteness, we associate with them the various impressions received by the eye, and learn to infer their distance in the use of this organ alone. Its informations, however, entirely depend on the previous *handling*. Without experience, sight would be perfectly helpless —as is proved by the fact, that persons born blind who have suddenly obtained their sight, cannot for some time even walk the streets. Every thing appears to them fixed in a plane, till repeated trials have taught them to correct the i lusion. Supposing therefore, a state of things, in which by reason of the great remoteness or inaccessibleness of objects, experiment is impossible: it is clear that sight would be forever at fault, and unable to form the least notion of the relations in space, which they bear to each other. Such was actually the state of the prophet. He had no measure by which to judge of the real size or proportion of the events he foresaw. He was ushered into a new world, nothing belonging to which he had ever *touched*—where all was etherial—boundless—"dark by excessive bright." Nothing in his own experience, or that of his nation, or of mankind at large, offered the slightest clue to guide him through the wondrous scene; as Isaiah distinctly commemorates, "From the beginning of the world men have not heard, nor perceived by the ear; neither hath the eye seen, O God, beside thee, what he hath prepared for him that awaiteth on him." No wonder that he was utterly lost in the comtemplation, and stood amazed—like the man blind from his birth, when his darkened eyeballs first open on the glories of the visible universe!

4th. As the scenes and events described were present to him, *so their dress and coloring were borrowed from objects, with which, as a Jew he was familiar.* The whole representation having the nature of a picture addressed to the eye, it was necessary that a certain system of imagery be adopted, in which the great moral truths should lie enshrined, as in a beautiful casket. This imagery must be familiar to him, and the people; otherwise it would be unintelligible.

Hence we find, that the kingdom of Christ is always exhibited by ideas taken from the national theocracy. Messiah is not only "Son of David," but "David" himself. Mount Zion and Jerusalem, the religious and civil metropolis of the nation, signify the Church redeemed by the blood of the only true sacrifice for sin, and serving God in spirit and in truth. The aggrandizement and enlargement of Jerusalem, are the enlargement and increase of that church. Her enemies are called by the names of the ancient enemies of Judah—Egypt, Ammon, Moab, Edom, and Babylon. The restoration of the Jews in latter days to the blessings of God's covenant, is symbolized by their rebuilding a temple on Mount Moriah: and the union of all nations in the love and worship of God, is shadowed forth by a universal participation in the feast of tabernacles. The extinction of sectarian feuds, and the delightful harmony prevailing among the lovers of the Lord Jesus Christ, especially the redeemed children of Abraham, is beautifully represented by the healing of the ancient separation between Israel and Judah.

There is nothing strange in this. It is perfectly natural to invest our conceptions with the hue appropriate to our physical and moral condition, and the objects with which we are daily conversant. Where could the prophet have gone, if precluded from this source of coloring? Besides, there was a most serious truth at the bottom. Our blessed Saviour tells us, that he came not to destroy the law, but to fulfil—in other words, that his religion is but the purification and expansion of the faith of God's ancient people. How entirely becoming then was it, that the spirit of prophecy should paint its future glory in those forms of thought, to which the people were accustomed, and which were so dear to the national heart!

These remarks have perhaps been unduly protracted. But the subject is important, and we think—not always understood. Besides, our statement of general principles, relieves from the necessity of entering into a minute detail of rules: two only shall be specified.

1st. *Be not anxious to find chronological connection and order in the prophecies.* They are all fragmentary, and exhibit their subject in detached pieces. We have also seen, that events the most widely separated in time, are grouped together, as if contemporary, or immediately following each other. Due regard to this, will enable us to dispense with many violent expedients which have been resorted to by the learned; especially with the irrational assumption of a "double sense" in prophecy. That which gave it favor with commentators, was the fact above stated, that events far separated in time, were closely connected in description—to explain which, they found it convenient to suppose two distinct fulfilments. The first, they imagined to take place in some event which occurred among the Jewish people, during the existence of their economy. The second and more perfect, was realized in the advent of the Saviour. To give the scheme greater respectability, it was married to Typology, who adopted the children as her own, calling the temporal fulfilment—the *type*, and the other the *antitype*. A good example occurs in the 10th and 11th chapters of Isaiah already quoted. The 10th, announces the destruction of the Assyrian empire. In the 11th, the prophet advances at once to the glories of the Messiah's reign—when "the wolf shall dwell with the lamb, and the leopard with the kid, and nothing shall hurt nor destroy, in all God's holy mountain." Yet not a few contend, that this magnificent prophecy had a primary fulfilment in Hezekiah; though they grant a far more complete accomplishment in our Redeemer, of whom we need not add that they suppose Hezekiah to have been a type!

The view is arbitrary beyond measure, and opposed to facts. We maintain without fear, that wherever Christ is definitely spoken of at all, he is spoken of *alone*, and where the blessedness of his rule is delineated, no other blessedness is delineated. Even in the Messianic Psalms, he is the *entire subject*. David may have gathered materials of his descriptions from incidents in his own life and experience, but in no proper sense does he speak of himself. His exalted "Lord" is the all in all which occupies his mind. When you meet therefore a passage, connecting at once the coming of a glorious epoch with the rebuilding of the temple after the Babylonish captivity, dismiss all anxiety to find it partially or typically fulfilled in Zerubbabel, or Alexander the great, or the Maccabees; but instantly transport yourselves into Messianic times, or, if necessary, to the consummation of all things. The notion that prophecy has two senses, a primary and secondary, throws a dark cloud of suspicion over both—almost conceding to the infidel, that it is a kind of writing which cannot be understood by the ordinary laws of exegesis. Above all, it is fatal to the argument drawn from this source in favor of the Gospel. When we advance a prediction from the Old Testament to establish the divine mission of Jesus, its whole proving force lies in this—that a series of events is announced, which was verified in him, and him alone. But if we discover a specific meaning in it which has no reference to him; the infidel by accepting it relieves himself from all pressure—reminding us of our discovery, and waving off the secondary and mystical senses we offer him, with a polite but peremptory "Credat Judæus Apella."

It is surprising to what length this mode of interpreting the Old Testament has been carried. Grotius may be quoted as an example, who does not find more than six passages in the whole volume, which immediately relate to the Saviour. On the other hand, he gives him the benefit of the second sense with princely liberality—as for instance in his commentary on the fifty-third chapter of Isaiah. He actually makes the wonderful personage there delineated, whose vicarious sufferings and glorious exaltation, after redeeming his people, are described with such strength of expression, and perfect accordance with the New Testament portraiture of Christ, that it seems rather history than prediction, to be the prophet *Jeremiah!!* He grants, indeed, at the commencement, that in "a more sublime sense," it applies to the Messiah: but that this is only a graceful bow—a "leaving his card with compliments," appears very clearly in the fact that he scarcely mentions him again, while "Jeremiah" stands out prominently in every verse. We confess that in reading such gallimatia, we can hardly repress a feeling of contempt towards the interpreter, or the author he expounds: and if we believed that the latter was *rightly* expounded, we would devoutly pray that he might be conveyed, as soon as possible, to the lumber-room of the antiquary, never again to see the light of the sun! Thus explained, the whole prophetic record, instead of being a buttress to Christianity, would be a "bowing wall and a tottering fence," which its enlightened advocate would be glad to see cleared away to the last stone!

Yet there are few errors in the world made up of pure falsehood, and even this contains something which entitles it to benefit of clergy. There are prophecies which, from their indefinite and general nature, admit manifold applications, and are not necessarily determined to one specific event. In other words, they contain, or are based on certain great *principles*, adopted by God in the government of the church and the world, which principles develop themselves in all appropriate circumstances. This is entirely different from the double sense referred to. The sense is *one:* but as with all general enunciations, there is a *pregnancy* in it which allows its fulfilment —not a second time merely, but a tenth, or if it please God, a thousandth. Thus, when he promises that after long chastising the daughter of Zion, he will return and heal her backsliding—that he will impart to her children true repentance for their sins, and establish, as of old, his throne in the midst of them—that their enemies shall be confounded, their number increased, the Gentile nations bow down before them, &c., we know that they are general truths—edicts of perpetual force, which, though spoken immediately in connection with a single event in history, have a far more extensive application. They will be *always verified*—though more strikingly at one period than another. The deliverance from Babylon, for instance, was part of a comprehensive scheme of divine wisdom and mercy, which ages before, wrought similar redemptions, and would unfold itself still more gloriously in the distant future.

We have here a beautiful feature of the divine government, well deserving our study. It does not proceed capriciously, or with a zigzag movement, like the schemes of men; but steadily onward, according to a few great ideas in the bosom of God; so that though a careless observer sees nothing around him but change and accident, there is really nothing that can be called new under the sun. The Messiah himself lived before his coming, in dark, shadowy resemblances—being the crowning realization of a great thought, that has been ever present to the divine mind, and shapes all its plans and purposes—the thought, that as man, by his own free will, produced the whole mass of evil under whose heavy weight he ceaselessly groans, so his victory over them must be achieved by himself. Suffering humanity is to find her deliverer *in her own lacerated bosom!* The drama of redemption opened in paradise with this proeme. In that first word of hope which cheered the hearts of our unhappy parents, by the assurance that their seed should "bruise the head" of their adversary, a principle was contained that did not sleep through the long interval of four thousand years, and then suddenly awakened, to usher in the great author of our spiritual redemption—but it put forth its living energy through every successive age, in those noble spirits, whose achievements in the cause of God and human happiness, proved that there was a power at work in the world greater than that of evil.

In this point of view, we admit, with a feeling very different from reluctance, that the prophecies of Messiah's day were also so many indirect *pointings* to events which preceded it, and bore to it a certain analogy, as expressions of one great law. As the terrible cataclysms which change the face of nature are usually introduced by strange appalling sounds and convulsive heavings, that may be called her sighs and notes of woe, in anticipation of the approaching catastrophe, so the jubilee of man's salvation had its glad precursors. The anthem sung by angels on the plains of Bethlehem at the advent of its glorious author, was not entirely new. Ten centuries before that memorable night, an ear open to celestial melodies might have heard its faint echo and reverberation on the same favored spot, at the birth of a royal man-child, in the cot of Jesse! So far, we are willing to go: all this, we lovingly embrace: but still retaining a mortal antipathy to the doctrine, as usually understood, of a "double sense."

2. *Do not interpret Prophecy too literally.* Its splendid imagery, and glowing pictures must not be tortured into statements, such as a witness makes in a court of justice, or a historian in describing the campaigns of Wellington, or Bonaparte: they are figures, and must be treated as figures. Here, our Millenarian Brethren err exceedingly. Their whole hypothesis of the Jews becoming pre-eminent as a nation over all the people of the earth, the actual subjugation of the latter under their political sway, the rebuilding of the temple, the resurrection of the martyrs, and the personal residence of Christ as a temporal monarch in Jerusalem, rests on no other basis than the assumption, that tropes when found in

the Bible tell the literal truth. It is the very error committed by the carnal Jews themselves, and which led to their rejection of the Just One. Inflated with the most fantastic hopes and anticipations nurtured by their mistaken interpretation of Prophetic symbols, they crucified their prince, not because he failed in proving his celestial mission, but because he had nothing to offer them, except a "kingdom, that was righteousness, peace and joy in the Holy Ghost."

To the instances already cited, proving that the imagery taken from the Theocracy was symbolical of great moral and spiritual truths, we add the following, merely as specimens: the student must pursue the investigation for himself. In the latter part of the 11th chapter of Isaiah, we have a magnificent account of the martial gathering of the Jews under the standard of the Messiah, and their brilliant conquests over enemies. The question is, whether we must understand it literally? Try the principle upon the 14th verse; "But they shall fly upon the shoulders (the figure is taken from the pouncing of a ravenous bird) of the Philistines toward the west; they shall lay their hand upon Edom and Moab, and the children of Ammon shall obey them." These were the ancient enemies of the theocracy, and are according to our view, selected by the Poet with great taste and appropriateness, as representatives of every thing opposed to the peace and happiness of the covenanted people, when they should have submitted themselves to

Christ. If wrong in this, we see no alternative but to expect along with a resurrection of the martyrs, that of all the savage clans who infested Israel during her national existence. Try it on the 15th verse: "The Lord shall utterly destroy the tongue of the Egyptian sea, and shake his hand over the river, and smite it in the seven streams, and make men go over dry shod." There is here, a beautiful allusion to the Exodus of Israel from Egypt through the Red Sea. On that occasion, God brought his people safely through the raging waters, but now—he promises that he will utterly destroy the sea itself. Can this mean any thing more, than that when his ancient people are to be gathered into the Christian fold, he will *remove every obstruction*; no obstacle shall be so great, that he will not put it out of the way by his almighty power.

In Hosea ii. 14, God promises that he will bring his church "into the wilderness, and speak comfortably to her as in the day when she came out of the land of Egypt, and give her vineyards and the valley of Achor for a door of hope." No one surely dreams, that the Jews are again to travel through Arabia Petræa, under the guidance of the fire and cloud. The words are plainly allusive, and express the general idea—that God will deliver his people from their spiritual bondage, and give them every proof of his cordial and tender love.

What shall be done with such a passage as that in

Malachi, which distinctly states that the old Prophet Elijah is to come from heaven, and announce the advent of the Messiah? "Behold I send Elijah the prophet before the coming of the great and dreadful day of the Lord." Nothing is more express; and the literalist would most certainly add to the accompaniments of the personal advent, a mission of this prophet, (as some have done,) if Christ had not determined him in Matthew xi. 14, to be John the Baptist. We are so happy in this case, as to have not only a New Testament interpretation of the phrase as applied to John, but a New Testament statement of the reason for it, which we take leave to employ as our key, in opening other dark chambers in ancient Prophesy. Luke i. 17: "He shall go in the *spirit and power* of Elias, to turn the hearts of the fathers to the children, and the disobedient to the wisdom of the just."

The 33d chapter of Jeremiah exhibits the principle for which we contend, in so clear and decisive a manner, that it is quite sufficient of itself to settle the question. God is promising to his people, the advent of their great spiritual Redeemer, and the happy consequences of his reign are graphically descibed in v. 15: "In those days will I cause the Branch to grow up unto David. In those days shall Judah be saved, and Jerusalem shall dwell safely; and this is the name wherewith she shall be called, The Lord our righteousness." That the Prophet is expatiating on the blessedness of the new economy in these words, is beyond a doubt. But what thought immediately follows? Surely, unless I apply my key, a very singular one: v. 18, "Neither (in these times) shall the Priests and Levites want a man before me *to offer burnt offerings, and to kindle meat offerings, and to do sacrifice continually.*" Is it possible to consider this as any thing more than symbol, borrowed from the Levitical service of the old economy? Will Aaron return from his grave; Christian altars rise to steam with the blood of rams, lambs, and he-goats; and the purified churches of the Redeemer return to those weak and beggarly elements from which she has been delivered? The fantastic notion got up to evade the force of many passages resembling this, that the Jews will return to their own land *unconverted*, and offer sacrifices, is of no service here. The Levitical bondage is expressly declared to be *enduring*, and its continuance is represented as one of the most glorious incidents of King Messiah's reign.

It is needless to dwell on a point so evident. The scheme of these ingenious gentlemen cannot stand It introduces a worldly element in our holy religion at utter variance with its genius and spirit. By its dazzling promises of "all the kingdoms of the earth and their glory," it strengthens the earthly principle within us, and greatly lowers the tone of Christian sentiment. It dishonors the glorified person of our Redeemer, by degrading him from the seventh heavens to our miserable earth, from the right hand of the Eternal Father, to a marble hovel in Jerusalem: and all this it does, not only without necessity, but in violation as we think of the plainest rules of sound interpretation.

With regard to the Apocalypse of John, we have made no special reference to it, as its highly figurative and allegorical character strikes every reader at once. Indeed it is surprising, that persons should be found capable even in their dreams, of putting literal constructions on any part of a book so decidedly and professedly enigmatical, with the exception of the first three chapters. Yet this is done to a certain extent by the expositors above mentioned, though they are far from carrying out the principle with due consistency. They grant all we are disposed to ask, concerning the general structure of the poem; for poem, beyond all doubt, it is. They allow, that its angels with their trumpets, sickles and vials—its thrones, four living creatures, and elders clothed in white—its "locusts," like horses prepared unto the battle—"its red dragon with seven heads and ten horns"—its woman "clothed with the sun" and that other female who "sits on many waters and is drunk with the blood of Saints," are parts of a splendid gallery of emblematic pictures, designed to represent certain great moral truths connected with the state and progress of the church in different ages. But when they come to the *Martyr's corner*, they suddenly wax literal—insisting that the "souls of them that were beheaded for the witness of Jesus," are the identical men and women who died at former periods, and are now to rise from their graves and reign with Christ in person, a thousand calendar years! This theory, they maintain in the face of two plain and undeniable facts; first, that the resurrection of the martyrs, stands in the very centre of the boldest symbolical imagery which the book contains; and secondly, that "*resurrection*" is a favorite figure employed by the Prophets, to denote any great moral renovation in general, and is used in cases where physical resuscitation is entirely out of the question. Isa. xxxvi. 19, Ezek. xxxvii. 13, Hos. vi. 2. Sober criticism would draw a conclusion directly opposite to that of these gentlemen—would infer that the phrase in question cannot possibly receive any other than a figurative sense, on the very rational and obvious principle, that a symbolical document must be *symbolically* interpreted.

While, however, we differ from the literalists; let us avoid the other extreme, that of turning Prophesy entirely into figure. Doubtless many things will take place, substantially as described. Such we think is the promised return of the Jews to their own land. We build the opinion, not so much on expressions used in the Prophets, which *might all be symbolical of their union* to *the spiritual theocracy*, as on the covenant stipulations given to the people in the land of Moab, and recorded in the 30th and 31st chapters of Deuteronomy. This legislative edict, which I have no right perhaps, to treat as a predictive poem, states most emphatically, and with great variety of phrase, that if after being rooted out of their country they should repent, the "Lord their God would bring them back int othe land, which their fathers possessed, and they should possess it." Still more confidently do we believe in their conversion to Christ, their holy brotherhood with the Gentiles, and the universal reign of peace on the earth. How far the literal fulfilment will be carried, we are ignorant. God did not give us prophecy, that we might know all things; but might have encouragements to faith, and incentives to holy exertion. The expositor who has not learnt to be ignorant—and to let his ignorance sit gracefully on him, has yet to learn the elements of his art.

RULE X.

Allow no interpretation, that will cast a shade of doubt over the perfect purity and truth of our Lord's teachings, or those of his Apostles. This may seem an unnecessarily pompous enunciation of something that is self-evident. But lamentable facts prove the contrary. Our German friends give us no little trouble with certain discoveries which they profess to have made in the Hermeneutics of the New Testament, and have invented or borrowed a theory, by which they contrive to rid themselves of every truth contained in it, that does not please them.

Its fundamental principle is this. Christ and his Apostles were noble spirits, who soared far above the level of their age, and with Plato, but more justly than Plato, might be called "heaven-born accidents." In a certain sense, but a fine and transcendental one which we do not stop to explain, they were even inspired. But they were also *Jews;* lived among Jews; their mission was to Jews, and like wise men, they took advantage of their situation. Not wishing to displease the people, and desirous of gaining admittance to their minds, they turned themselves into thorough-going Rabbis—indulging in all those fanciful opinions and speculations, which were so admired by their countrymen. Thus, they had a complete science of angelology, and demonology. Christ adopted it, and when mad or epiletic persons were brought to him, he said that they were possessed with "*demons.*" They believed that when Messiah came, he would raise the just from their graves. He humored them in this also, and taught the "*Resurrection:*" borrowing with the same freedom their notion of a great subterranean vorago, in whose sulphureous flames the wicked should be eternally tormented.

This principle is unsparingly applied to the use which he and his disciples make of the Old Testament. Indeed, it is from this source its supporters draw their arguments, almost exclusively. The mystical and allegorical mode of expounding—the wish to find recondite meanings in the simplest passages and even in the arrangement of words and letters, had become, it is alleged, a perfect mania, to which grammar, logic, and common sense were sacrificed without remorse. To this mode of teaching the wise Redeemer conformed. We are not to look therefore for any solidity in the arguments he employs from the Old Testament. It is enough, that his ultimate conclusions are found correct, after *a careful sifting*—the premises being nothing more than "argumenta ad hominem," which suited the people of that time and place, but have no force in the present day, at least for gentlemen who have passed through the curriculum scientiarum, in the university of Leipsic or Gottingen.

This is the famous doctrine of "Accommodation,"—"Condescension,"—"Wise Œconomy," which prevails on the European continent, and with which the neologist performs such marvels in exegesis. Its meaning cannot be mistaken. The sacred writers of the New Testament cared not a straw for the oceans of falsehood and nonsense they slavered forth, if they only struck the fancy of those whom they wished to make Christians. They were the Father Jesuits of those days, who regarded not the means, if the end was good, and spared no arts of chicanery that would promote their object. It is really surprising, that men calling themselves Christian divines, should under any temptation resort to a scheme so fatal to all trust in divine revelation; and which charges our blessed Redeemer with a policy, that would disgrace the scurviest demagogue, that ever mounted a stump, to entertain with *bunkum* an ignorant half-drunken mob! Had he pursued it, he would not have been a teacher for Hottentots, and, in a short time, would have been cast off by his warmest admirers, in consequence of finding that they could not depend on anything he said. Lie number *one*, they could have endured perhaps, from grateful feelings to a teacher who betrayed such anxiety to please them. But who could bear a succession of lies, or attend a course of instruction based on lying? Strange as the thing may seem, these gentlemen could do it; for with a recklessness that can be only explained by the tendency of certain studies exclusively pursued, to demoralize the intellect and blunt its perception of the difference between right and wrong, they justify the practice; contending that it is nothing more than a fair application of the "argumentum ad hominem."

There is no truth in their assertion. That the "argumentum ad hominem," in other words, the assumption of the false opinion of one whom we seek to convince is allowable in certain cases, may be admitted; though of all modes of reasoning it is the last which a lofty mind would resort to, unless the object proposed was action, rather than conviction. But there is a limitation which no man of the least self-respect will neglect. The person to be convinced must *understand* his teacher—that he is not *teaching*, but removing obstructions, and using the errors and false opinions which darken his mind, for no other purpose but to prepare him for the truth. There is not indeed always a necessity of explicit statement, for the true intent may be gathered from attending circumstances—or the avowal of it may be deferred to another occasion. But sooner or later it must appear, and certainly will appear, if the teacher has any higher object in view than to bewilder and mislead some poor simpleton whom he has selected to be the victim of his superior ingenuity. Above all, we demand this from a religious instructor who declares that he comes from God to enlighten the moral darkness of the soul. To imagine the contrary—to suppose that the great Being would allow his ambassador to furnish the child of immortality with a chart full of errors and false directions, no matter what may be the pretext, is to suppose that he has usurped the throne of the Devil, and robbed him of his proper paternity: Satan can no more claim to be the "father of lies!" This may be called declamation, rather than argument; but it is the only way of treating the subject. Morality is a thing not to be established by reasoning, nor is false morality to be refuted by it. Both are the objects of pure intuitive perception—and when a fundamental error is committed, all that remains is to place it vividly, and distinctly before the mind.

We have said, that the principal support which they find for their theory, is the way in which Christ and his Apostles quote the Old Testament. The remarks that follow shall therefore be mainly directed to this point, and will make the falsehood of their allegations level to the comprehension of a child.

The quotations in the Gospel from the Old Testament, are of two kinds; first, The *Rhetorical*, as we choose to call them, the design of which is to illustrate; secondly, the *Logical*, which aims to instruct, and convince. These must be carefully separated, though the friends of accommodation evince great care in endeavoring to confound them.

The *Rhetorical* use of the Old Testament, consists in the employment by Christ and his apostles of its ideas and expressions, to impart vivacity and force to their own conceptions. From very early times, the Jews glowed with a love and veneration for their sacred books, of which we can scarcely form an idea. They were their pride, their delight, their constant study—combining in one, all their civil polity, history, literature, and religious faith. They sang them, they prayed in them, they carried them to their fasts and their feasts, to their marriages, and funeral solemnities, to their courts of law, to their temple, and their synagogues. Let the reader imagine if he pleases, all our books of poetry and prose, of geography, law, science, and theology fused and amalgamated into a single volume, he will form an exceedingly faint conception of that which his Scriptures were to a son of Abraham, eighteen hundred years ago. Is it surprising then, that they should become an inexhaustible treasury of thoughts, phrases, sentiments, on which they drew when under the influence of deep emotion? This they would do, without troubling themselves with nice questions about the exact meaning of what they quoted. Man is something more than a reasoning machine,—a mere grinder of syllogisms. He is not always with square in hand, taking the dimensions of a pyramid, nor demonstrating the relation between cosines and tangents. He feels joy and sorrow, fear and love,—soars in hope, or creeps in despondency. In such cases, how pleasant to the man of taste and reading, that he can pour out his heart in the words of some favorite author! The products of his own mind are entirely too mean, to be the vehicle of expression for the strong emotions pent up within; and he borrows the wings of his bard, whose glorious creations have become so entwined with every fibre of his soul, that he scarcely recognizes them as another's, but treats them as part of his own living self.

Thus was it with the Jew, and thus with the Jewish Saviour, and his Jewish apostles. Is it in the least wonderful then, that a rich poetical coloring should be spread over all their conceptions; that whenever they opened their mouth, there would drop lilies and roses called from the fair garden where they spent their happiest hours, communing with God and their own pure and holy thoughts? In such utterances, there was nothing studied or sought after. The idea before their minds called up by natural association some passage from the Old Testament; which required no bidding to make its appearance, and was thrown out in illustration of the principal thought, with graceful artlessness. Nor was it necessary that the correspondence between them should be real, and intimate. Nothing more was required than such a degree of resemblance, (perhaps merely verbal) as would please the fancy, and enliven the sentiment to be expressed.

In this way the fact is explained, that there are in the New Testament no less than nine hundred references to its venerable sister, most of which belong to the class under our notice. We gave some examples in discussing our seventh Rule, and they must not be multiplied. Let the Reader turn back to them for a moment, and he will need no additional illustrations. The first will fully answer his purpose: "A voice in Rama, lamentation and great mourning, Rachel weeping for her children, and refusing to be comforted," Matt. ii. 18. Most certainly, the Prophet Jeremiah from whom this is cited, did not predict the massacre in Bethlehem; but describes a scene that occasioned in his own time, six hundred years before the birth of the Saviour. Yet there was a distant resemblance, which to the mind of Matthew, steeped as it was in Bible memories, might occur very naturally. Indeed, there is in the greater number of these quotations, (viewed from the rhetorical standpoint, as our German friends would say,) a tasteful appropriateness which must strike every mind.

But secondly, Our writers did not always employ their Jewish recollections in this way. As ambassadors of heaven, they had a serious work to perform, which would not allow them to be always walking among flowers, or gathering shells on the sea shore. As teachers of divine truth, expounders of the way of salvation, they were to address frequently the pure intellect of men, convincing them by "sound speech which could not be condemned," that the message they brought was not a cunningly-devised fable. Here too, they recur to the good old book. But the design is different. It is no more regarded as a cabinet of gems and golden ornaments, but a treasure-house of arguments by which their countrymen may be brought to the feet of the Saviour—the garden becomes an armory, and every word of citation belongs to the "company of valiant men standing round the bed of Solomon, all having swords and expert in war!" In these cases, we repel the changes of our opponents with indignant earnestness, affirming that in every instance the Old Testament is quoted, according to its true intent and meaning.

If it be asked, how we may determine the class to

which a passage belongs, we are compelled to say that none of the formulas usually employed for marking a quotation, will be of much assistance. The expression, "that it might be fulfilled," "as the scripture saith," &c., merely point out a general correspondence without explainiug its nature, and may undoubtedly be prefixed to either class, though some interpreters have attempted to make distinctions. There is however no practical difficulty in settling questions of this kind. After reading the passage, let the student ask himself: Is the sacred writer *reasoning here*? Is the text part of a chain of argument which he is evidently carrying on either to instruct a pupil, or convict a gainsayer? Is he occupying the domain of intellect,—or of fancy, and feeling? Let him do this, and we promise that he shall not find more than six passages in the New Testament, that will give him serious trouble. Of the facility with which the principle can be applied, take one or two examples.

In Acts ii. 17, the Apostle Peter defending himself and associates from the charge of drunkenness, tells the Jews that the excitement they witnessed (on the day of Pentecost) was really the work of God's holy Spirit, and distinctly predicted by the prophet Joel, "But this is that spoken by the prophet Joel; and it shall come to pass in those days, I will pour out my spirit," &c. There can be no doubt respecting the class to which this belongs. Peter is arguing a solemn and weighty point with professed unbelievers.

If his appeal to Joel was a false one, and that it would be, if Joel did not refer to the very transaction that was going on, Peter was guilty of a fraud or a folly, which deprived him of all right to be respected as a teacher. That he was right, and that the prediction does refer to Gospel times, is universally admitted by fair and honest critics. In the same chapter, another striking instance occurs. Speaking of the resurrection of Christ, which his unbelieving audience of course denied, he quotes a paragraph from Psalm xvi. which asserts concerning some one, that "God would not leave his soul in hades, or suffer his holy one to see corruption." This personage, the Apostle in an elaborate argument, shows could not be David, and concludes in the 31st verse, "David seeing this before, spake of the resurrection of Christ, that his soul was not left," &c. Here again we say, that if the passage in the Old Testament does not mean precisely what the apostle says it meant, his character is gone forever: we question whether miracle could have saved it. As interpreters, therefore, we are bound to show that the 16th Psalm is prophetic of Messiah, which can be triumphantly done.

One other example. When we open the epistle to the Hebrews, we find it commences with an earnest argument for the divinity of Christ. It begins at the 5th verse, and consists of no less than seven allegations from the Old Testament. Now it cannot be possible that these are merely rhetorical. If, on so grave and momentous a theme, the author put off his readers with a motley collection of Rabbinical conceits, the credit of his whole epistle would have been utterly ruined in the esteem of every honest man. That he has not done so, but on the contrary, that he has treated his authorities with logical fairness and accuracy, could easily be evinced.

Our remarks have been directed exclusively to the use made by our Lord and his Apostles of the Old Testament for the reason assigned, viz., that our opponents draw their principal arguments from this source. With regard to the sanction of other Jewish errors, but one example can be alleged with any plausibility: we refer to the belief in demoniac possession. It certainly appears singular, that evil spirits should have been allowed to exercise so terrible a power over the bodies of men in one particular age of the world, exclusive of all succeeding times: and the symptoms resemble so closely those of insane and epileptic persons, that if any safe expedient were found for maintaining that Christ did not intend to teach the doctrine, we should be tempted to adopt it. But this seems impossible. The way in which he always treats the subject—his conversations with the demons—the various circumstances accompanying the cure, and the impression uniformly made upon the spectators, absolutely preclude the idea that he employed the Jewish notion rhetorically, or in such a manner as to leave it doubtful whether he himself believed it. We therefore accept the doctrine as part of his authoritative teachings—earnestly advising our young friends not to indulge a habit of thinking in relation to it, that may lead them to the verge of a precipice, from which it will not be easy to retrace their steps.

If, unfortunately, a man cannot bring himself to unite with us in the acceptance, we would remind him that he does far less dishonor to the character of Jesus, by holding that he taught an error, *believing it to be truth*, than by asserting that he taught it—*knowing its falsehood.* Perhaps such a view does not necessarily invalidate his authority as a religious teacher. Jesus, it might be said, was a *man;* and the mysterious union with a higher nature, did not establish such an actual communication between the Divine and Human, that he in the latter capacity exercised the prerogative of omniscience. The true pathology of disease might have been hidden from him, as the other secrets of science—those of chemistry for instance; and thus, as he changed water into wine without being acquainted with the elementary molicules which compose the two fluids, he might have healed diseases with the same imperfect knowledge of their causes which characterized his age.

We have no liking to this hypothesis. The doctrine of demoniac agency has too many points of contact with fundamental questions in morality and religion, to be considered a mere scientific error; and the supposition that our blessed Redeemer should be the victim of delusion on a point so momentous, is abhorrent to all our Christian instincts. Our only object in suggesting it, is to affirm, that it approaches infinitely nearer Christian faith than the villanous doctrine of "accommodation." The man of piety however, stands in no need of it. At best, the scheme is a perilous one, however it may claim the praise of harmlessness when compared with a worse. Let us on a subject so entirely belonging to the invisible world, and beyond the range of our present faculties, cast theory to the winds—cherishing the pleasant and surely not irrational belief, that at a certain period in the world's history, the holy Providence of God suffered a temporary unloosing of the powers of evil, to grace the advent of their mighty and divine Conqueror!

On the whole, no student of his Bible has the least reason to fear any evil consequences from the most severe and searching examination of the topic which we have been considering. The assertions of our opponents are much stronger than their arguments—and their boldness exceeds their discretion. Deep reverence for God—a cultivated moral sense—and above all, a habitual contemplation of the perfect model of purity, truth, and excellence furnished us in the character of the great Author of our religion, with a respectable degree of learning, will be an effectual safeguard, unless counteracted by external influences, and that greatest of all calamities, a naturally cold and sceptical temperament.

RULE XI.

We must endeavor to obtain reasonable certainty that the printed text gives the true reading of our book; and for this purpose, must study and apply the art of Criticism. That so ancient a volume as the Bible should have come down to us perfectly free from error, is a supposition too absurd to be reasoned with. The fact is, no two manuscripts of the eight hundred that have been examined, entirely agree; and as each has a claim to be heard, we must often be at a loss in passing judgment on their discrepancies. A knowledge, therefore, of the principles according to which such questions should be decided, with ability to use it, is indispensable. We have no right to exercise a blind and lazy faith in others, however eminent—but in every case must be qualified, in some degree, to judge for ourselves. The science which teaches these things is called *Criticism*; and thus we say, that every interpreter must be to a certain extent, a *critic.* He must acquaint himself with the history of the text in different ages, with the number and probable age of the different manuscripts, their notation and comparative value, with the various theories of the learned concerning their classification, with ancient versions, and with the "canons," as they are called, by which the intrinsic excellence of readings is judged, in the absence or defect of external evidence.

Unfortunately for this study, a bad odor has been given to it by a school of thinkers in Germany, who have carried their critical speculations beyond all bounds of common sense, and even decency. Catching the spirit of inquiry which, sixty years ago, began to separate truth from error in classical history and literature, they with reckless ardor directed it to the Christian revelation. Establishing themselves as the Wolfs and Niebuhrs of this new region, they soon began to doubt the integrity of large portions of scripture, on the ground of what they called the "Higher Criticism;"—this Higher Criticism being a sort of inward light, enabling its possessor to distinguish between the genuine and the spurious by simple perception—in direct opposition to manuscripts, versions, uniform tradition, and every other accredited source of evidence. One doubt prepared the way for another, doubt ripened into denial; and so the work of mutilation has been going on, until our Bible has become a thing of shreds and patches, the like of which has been never seen in the shape of a written document.

But all this is no argument against the true Critical art, which consists in a searching, yet sober examination of the text, according to fixed laws, and with sacred regard to the maxim laid down by the illustrious Griesbach, "Let nothing be changed from conjecture." The fear of danger from such studies is unworthy of a Christian man. It implies a cowardly suspicion that something is rotten at the foundation, when examination would prove the soundness of every beam—and that not a stone of the least importance to the building is displaced. Our religion, blessed be God, is not a trumped-up fable! It came to do a great work in the world, and the evidence of that wonderful book in which it is recorded shall continue while earth endures. What a host of opposition has it not already overcome? Judaism fell before it in forty years. In three centuries, it rose on the ruins of Paganism to the empire of the civilized world. It survived the arts and oppressions of Antichrist. The Atheistic conspiracy which rose up against it in Europe half a century since, it laughed to scorn. Yearly, it is extending its triumphs over new regions. And after all, shall it fear to *have its papers searched?* Shall it quail before a score or two of pragmatical Germans, who, whatever be their learning and one-sided acuteness, give slender proof of that large comprehensiveness of vision which distinguished a Bacon and a Locke, with a thousand others, who after the most brilliant achievements in science, were proud to lay their honors at its feet!

Had our good fathers in the seventeenth century made these reflections, they would have avoided a sad blunder. Instead of raising a senseless clamor against such men as Capellus, Wetstein, Mill, and Walton, who led the way in examining critically the text of scripture; they would have hailed their labors as invaluable contributions to Christianity. We confess that we never recall their history without a feeling of shame. With talents, and a force of character that would have raised them to eminence in any pursuit, they chose—instead of roaming through the flowery fields of the classics, to labor at the obscure task of defecating the word of God from its numerous blots and excrescences. They hid themselves in their studies as in prison cells, and delved for thirty years among old musty half effaced manuscripts which could not be decyphered without the aid of microscopes; collating one with another, comparing word with word and letter with letter; occasionally, they would devour by way of pastime the folio of an old Greek and Latin father, and after more than half a lifetime of such drudgery, they came forth with the momentous results—to be received with universal execration! Instead of being thanked for discovering the many faults of the received text, they were charged with being themselves corrupters of the pure word of God. Even the excellent John Owen entirely lost his temper, and told them that "they would have acted a wiser part if they had buried their discoveries in the earth, and never suffered a various reading to see the light. What a bulk and heap," he exclaims, "are they swelled to! The collection of them makes up a heap bigger than the Bible, and whither this work may yet grow I know not. Taking them altogether, I cannot but look on them as an engine suited to the destruction of the truth, and as a fit weapon put into the hands of men of atheistical principles such as this age abounds in, to oppose the whole evidence of truth revealed in the scriptures. I fear that Romanism or Atheism will be found to lie at the door."

This is a doleful paragraph. It is really sad to think of such a man as Owen—the prince of orthodox polemics—the irrefragable Doctor—"glorious John," making such a fool of himself—ready to give up the ghost in mortal agony, because Brian Walton and his associates are wearing out their very lives in the endeavor to provide him with a good New Testament! To think of such a gallant war-horse, whose neck was clothed with thunder in presence of an enemy, being thrown into a perfect frenzy of terror at the sight of a few honest friends, engaged in winnowing his provender! If the principles of such men had been adopted, it is easy to tell the consequences. There would have been an end to free investigation on the most important and fundamental points in theology. Mill and Walton would have been served with an injunction from the Lord Chancellor! Ignorance would have ex cluded forever enlightened certainty! Dr. Owen would have burnt all the manuscripts to prevent their blabbing, and what in this case would the evidence be worth, that the original documents of our faith had come down unimpaired!

Happily, those who undertook the work of emendation were not men of straw. It advanced bravely, and the result has been a glorious accession to the proofs of Christianity, which its warmest friends could scarcely anticipate. Of the mass of various readings collected, not one hundredth part in the least degree affects the sense. They consist almost wholly of minute grammatical differences, slight transpositions or substitutions of one particle for another, so trifling that one is apt to wonder how they came to be noticed. The question of substantial incorruptness is now put to rest, and will probably never be revived. That Religion will continue to receive benefit from critical investigations, we have not a doubt. Human learning in all its forms—even the most unsanctified, shall contribute to strengthen the foundations of our holy and beautiful temple, and Zion shall, according to the promise, be enriched with the spoils of her enemies!

This is not prediction merely, for it is already true. The lover of his Bible, when he sits down to examine the subject, will be surprised to find how little has been really accomplished by the bold innovators of the day. On the contrary, many difficulties have been removed, and dark places made plain. Certainty has been given to what formerly was wished—and hoped, rather than known, truth separated from error, and her friends enlightened as to the best way of defending her. Many of the learned who have distinguished themselves by the *looseness their speculations, are beginning to see* that they have gone too far, and are retracing their steps. Some have even made a public recantation, and are vigorous champions of the faith which once they persecuted.

We dwell on this subject at some length, because we fear that prejudices still linger among us, which ought to be corrected. Our desire is, to vindicate a most important branch of theological learning—and to convince our young friends, that if disposed to prosecute it in their private reading, they may do so without serious danger. But were the danger ever so imminent still they *must prosecute it.* The religious teacher is not at liberty in the matter—more than the soldier is at liberty to decline facing the enemy, because he may be shot! It is a proposition entirely self-evident, that if Christianity be defended from those who are scattering around fire-brands, arrows, and death, it can only be done by a thorough investigation of all those topics that are employed against it. Criticism is one of those poisons, to which there is no other antidote but the poison itself. It is like the fire of Phæton, which Jupiter could only extinguish by the fire of his thunder.

"Ignes compescuit ignibus."

If a phalanx of erudite German neologists attack the

authenticity of the Pentateuch—telling us that it was forged by some obscure priest during or after the Babylonian captivity, that the greater part of Isaiah was written long after his death, that large portions of Matthew, Luke, and John are interpolations, that the epistle to the Hebrews must be stricken from the Canon, and that the Apocalypse was written by a half-crazed Gnostic—something more must be done than groaning—knitting the brows—or hurling at them an "exorciso te scelestissime." The Christian minister must stand up to them and play the *man*—not the *ostrich*, who on the approach of an adversary, shuts his eyes and runs away—screaming!

After all that has been said, truth and candor require us to make a concession. We are far from asserting that the study of criticism will make no change in the views of a student nourished in the traditional belief. Let it be remembered, that the subjects of which it treats, have not until lately received thorough examination; while our systems and catechisms were framed long before. Now it would be passing strange, if no new light was reflected on them by the labors of so many learned. He must calculate therefore, on being occasionally compelled to modify his former opinions. Perhaps he thinks at present, that every word contained within the two boards of the New Testament that lies on his table, is indited by the Spirit of God, and would look with horror on the man who affirms that 1 John v. 7 is an interpolation. His notions may not always be so severe. He is sure that Paul wrote the epistle to the Hebrews. Perhaps he will discover, that though certainly written by an apostolical man, yet a doubt concerning its Pauline origin should not bring down the greater excommunication. He will also find that some books, 2 Peter and 2d and 3d John for instance, have not the full evidence of authenticity possessed by the others, and will feel the propriety of deducting a little from that unlimited confidence he would otherwise repose in them.

But who will say, that he ought not to change his views when they are clearly seen to be prejudices of education? The fear that a modification in things small and unessential may lead to an upturning of the whole system of belief, is most groundless. The very contrary is the fact; for by separating truth from the chaff which has been mingled with it, he sees more clearly its evidence, and can defend it with greater efficiency and success. If the writer were permitted to give a small leaf from the book of his own experience, he would say, that not a week passes over his head, in which he does not find reason to correct some partial or erroneous notion, that he had received he knows not how—and without examination. But so far from unsettling great fundamental principles, he invariably finds that his conviction is strengthened by every successive change. The number of Christian disciples is very small, who would not find their advantage, in subjecting their religious opinions to the same course of treatment which the great lord of the vineyard adopts toward his fruit-bearing branches: "He *purgeth* them, that they may bring forth more fruit."

www.ingramcontent.com/pod-product-compliance
Lightning Source LLC
LaVergne TN
LVHW050521100826
845148LV00002B/407